Criminal Justice
An Overview of the System

Adam J. McKee

Booklocker.com, Inc.
2016

http://www.docmckee.com/OER/

Criminal Justice

Adam J. McKee

Table of Contents

Preface

Most people have gained some understanding of how the American criminal justice system works simply by living in our society and being exposed to popular culture. Unfortunately, this common knowledge is incomplete and intermixed with many myths. Many important elements of our criminal justice system are simply not a part of the "average Joe's" understanding of how the system works. This text is designed to provide the reader with a clear and concise overview of the entire American criminal justice system with an eye to dispelling some common myths.

This book is organized around the various steps in the criminal justice system, describing the elements of the system that deal with those steps along the way. Of course, not every case will follow a neat, linear progression through the system. It must be remembered that the progression suggested herein is to some degree an oversimplification of the process. Due to our federal system of government, criminal cases are handled on the local, state, and federal levels. Each of these jurisdictions will vary to some degree from the next.

This text is a work in progress. To keep costs for students low, much of the traditional editing of a published work has been omitted. Accordingly, I am more than happy to consider suggestions for improvement for future editions as well as corrections to my grammar, usage, and style. I hope you find this book useful and informative, despite its several flaws. Please send comments and corrections to mckee@uamont.edu. Positive comments and adoption notifications are also welcome.

Chapter 1: The Criminal Justice System

One of the most important advantages to living in a civil society is the security that it provides. In contemporary society, the role of ensuring security is relegated to government. That is, citizens have a reasonable expectation that society, as a collective, will protect us from rogue members. In giving power to government to perform this critical security function, we create the potential for the abuse of that power. In the American system of criminal justice, we see two competing and equally important ideas: We demand both security and freedom from governmental abuse of power. These freedoms are collectively known as **individual rights** or **civil liberties**. These civil rights are woven into the very fabric of our government at both the state and federal level.

In this context, we can view the **criminal justice system** is a collection of rules and people (usually in the form of public agencies) working together to protect the public from harm. These elements are commonly divided into three broad categories: police, courts, and corrections. These three elements have the same basic function: To respond to crime. A **crime** is a violation of some criminal law with no legal justification or excuse. Local, state, and federal governments can make criminal laws. The vast majority of criminal laws are a matter of state **statutes**.

Saying that the criminal justice system has the purpose of "responding to crime" results in a dramatically oversimplified view of how the system works. Every agency within the criminal justice system will agree that it responds to crime, but we find profoundly different mission statements, goals, objectives, and methods among these myriad agencies. A major reason for these differences is that the public has several conflicting definitions of the concept of **justice**.

Section 1.1: Major Components of the Criminal Justice System

Learning Objectives

After completing this section, you should be able to:

1.1(a) Describe the differences between the individual rights and public order perspective.
1.1(b) Describe the need for a system of order maintenance within society and explain the role of law within that system.
1.1(c) Explain the structure of the criminal justice system in terms of the three major components using the vocabulary of criminal justice.
1.1(d) Understand the goals of the criminal justice system.
1.1(e) Describe how justice can be defined from various perspectives.

Introduction

In reality, there is no one criminal justice system in the United States. There are many similar systems. Each state has its criminal justice system, and the Federal government has another still. This section considers how these various systems are composed by looking at the major components common to them all. Traditionally, the criminal justice system can be divided into three major components: Police, Courts, and Corrections.

It may seem that there is no real common thread to this system. In the United States, the thing that binds all of the components together and regulates them is the **rule of law**. Philosophically, the rule of law is the idea that every person is subject to the law, even those that make the law, interpret the law, and enforce the law. The most potent law in the United States is the Constitution of the United States. This body of laws provides all Americans with civil liberties that the government cannot violate. If a state law or federal law violates any of these protections, then the courts will declare the law void. It is up to the appellate courts, most notably the Supreme Court, to interpret these laws and determine the exact nature and scope of specific civil liberties in the United States. Further, if an agent of the state or federal government violates a person's rights, that person has remedies available. For example, citizens can sue government employees that violate their rights under Section 1983 of the **United States Code**. An important remedy in criminal justice is the **exclusionary rule**. The exclusionary rule was established by the Supreme Court to prevent police misconduct. The rule states that illegally obtained evidence (evidence obtained in violation of someone's constitutional rights) cannot be admitted as evidence in court.

Police

People tend to use the word **police** generically to indicate those individuals with law enforcement responsibility. The majority of these are municipal police officers, but there are many **sheriffs' deputies** as well as state and federal agents that do not technically fit under the umbrella term "police." It is important to realize that enforcing the law is only a small fraction of what the police do every day. They maintain order and provide many services to the communities they serve. The police also have the responsibility of investigating crimes, collecting evidence, and work with prosecutors to obtain convictions in court.

The police are often called the "gatekeepers of the criminal justice system." This description is accurate because entry into the system requires formal action on the part of law enforcement. Police officers have incredible decision-making authority when dealing with citizens and suspects. An officer can choose to ignore an offense, issue a verbal warning, issue a written warning, issue a citation, or formally arrest the person. Of course, the seriousness of the crime plays a major role in how the police exercise **discretion**. An officer would not ignore or issue a citation to a person engaged in a serious felony crime.

The duties of police officers can be very general in the case of a patrol officer, or they can be very specialized, for example, in the case of a homicide detective. The level of specialization depends largely on the size of the agency where the officer works. Large, urban police departments tend to have more resources, more officers, and a higher degree of specialization. Despite this fact, the backbone of policing is the patrol division, and patrol is always a generalist function. The successful patrol officer is a jack-of-all-trades.

Courts

When law enforcement and prosecutors accuse a person of violating a criminal law, it is up to the courts to determine if the person did indeed violate the law. If so, it is up to the court prescribe the appropriate punishment (within the scope of the sentencing laws in that court's jurisdiction). Because the American legal system is **adversarial** in nature, there must always be two teams in any court case. In a criminal matter, a lawyer known as the **prosecutor** presents the government's case. A major goal of the prosecutor is to see the **defendant** found guilty of the alleged crime. To use a sports analogy, the prosecutor is the offense. The **defense attorney** has the job of trying to show that the defendant is not guilty, or at least that defendants should not be accountable for their actions for some legal reason. To continue the sports analogy, the **judge** serves as a referee, making sure that both sides diligently follow the rules of the "game." The **jury** is tasked with watching the game and deciding (at the end) who the winner is. In the adult criminal justice system, all cases are adversarial in nature. This point will prove to be important repeatedly as the workings of the criminal justice system are examined.

In a jury trial, the jury serves as the **finder of fact**. The term *finder of fact* in this case means that the jury decides whether the defendant is innocent or guilty. In serious cases, the defendant has a right to **trial by jury**. It is allowable, however, that the defendant consent to a bench trial. A bench trial is a trial where the judge takes on the role of the jury as finder of fact.

The term **courts**, used as a general heading, covers a wide array of professionals. It includes defense attorneys (both public servants and private contractors), prosecuting attorneys, judges, and court staff.

Corrections

Corrections is another umbrella term that is difficult to define because it encompasses so many diverse criminal justice activities. Corrections can include **probation**, **parole**, jail, prison, and myriad community-based sanctions that are becoming more and more popular. Another problem with accurately defining corrections is a general disagreement about the philosophy of **incarceration**. Does society send people to prison *as* punishment, or *for* punishment? Do we expect prisons to punish or rehabilitate? Most people can agree on one thing: The public expects correctional institutions to ensure the public safety.

A discussion of corrections usually begins with **jails**. Jails are usually operated at the local level, most often under the leadership of a **county sheriff**. Jails hold several different classifications of prisoners. Jails are most commonly thought of as holding individuals that have been arrested and are awaiting a first appearance in court. Legally, these individuals are presumed innocent because they have not been proven guilty. Other jail inmates have been convicted of relatively minor offenses (misdemeanors) and (in most states) are serving sentences of less than one year. Other prisoners may have been convicted of serious offenses, and are housed in the local jail awaiting transfer to a state prison.

Persons convicted of serious crimes can be sentenced to a **prison** term. A prison is generally larger, more secure, and provides more services than a jail. The reason for these extra services is that prisons are designed for long sentences (relative to jail sentences). Prisons are most often run at the state level of government, but there are also many federal prisons.

Defining Justice

One of the overarching goals that brings the components of the criminal justice system together is that each is designed (in some way) to promote justice. Everyone has an idea of what **justice** is, but pinning down a definition that will be widely agreed upon proves to be a challenge. There are several different ways of looking at the idea. One way to view justice is in terms of *equality*. In economic language, equality means that everyone gets the same amount, regardless of what they "put in." Another perspective is to view justice in terms of *equity*. When viewed this way, it means that people get what they deserve. In terms of economic reward, those "just deserts" are based on how hard the person works. When it comes to harms done to society, many feel that "just deserts" means that criminal punishments should be in proportion to the harm done. This concept of **just deserts** in criminal justice has been referred to as **retributive justice**. The idea of wrongdoers being deserving of repayment in kind is known by the Latin phrase *Lex Talionis*, or the law of retribution. In its purest form, *lex talionis* is the Biblical doctrine of "an eye for an eye, a tooth for a tooth." In today's criminal justice system, the idea of retribution takes on the meaning of variable lengths of prison sentences.

Both of the above definitions focus on the outcome of an act to determine if it was just. Another way to look at the idea of justice is to examine the process. In other words, an act is just if it was done using a fair process. Justice viewed in terms of fair process is often referred to as **procedural justice**. This idea leaves room for debate as to what sort of processes are to be considered fair. Accessibility and predictability are common criteria. In the United States, the idea of procedural justice is closely tied to the idea of **due process**. In a philosophical sense, due process means that agents of the criminal justice system conduct criminal proceedings in a "fundamentally fair" way. In a practical sense, due process means that the state must respect all legal rights of accused persons. What criminal justice procedures are required under due process is a dynamic body of rules. These rules are most often judicial determinations of what exactly the Constitution means in practice. The idea of due process is represented throughout the **Bill of Rights**, as well as being specifically guaranteed by both the **Fifth Amendment** (applies to the federal government) and the **Fourteenth Amendment** (applies to state government). Throughout this text, these fundamental civil liberties will be discussed in the context of the different elements of the criminal justice system. Police, courts, and corrections must all observe the legal requirements of due process.

Amendment V

No person shall be held to answer for a capital, or otherwise infamous crime, unless on a presentment or indictment of a grand jury, except in cases arising in the land or naval forces, or in the militia, when in actual service in time of war or public danger; nor shall any person be subject for the same offense to be twice put in jeopardy of life or limb; nor shall be compelled in any criminal case to be a witness against himself, **nor be deprived of life, liberty, or property, without due process of law**; nor shall private property be taken for public use, without just compensation.

Note that the Fifth Amendment is constructed in the form of a very, very long sentence. Many different subjects are addressed in that sentence. This type of sentence construction is common in the Constitution. When lawyers and legal scholars want to point out a particular phrase within that long sentence, they refer to it as a clause. The text specifying that no person shall **"be deprived of life, liberty, or property, without due process of law"** is known as the **due process clause.** Some fundamental liberties are expressed in the constitution in this manner. Other rights, however, are not explicitly stated in the constitution. The due process clause is of critical importance to civil liberties because it stands in as a proxy for many other rights. The right to privacy, for example, is never specifically mentioned in the Constitution. Such a right exists, according to the Supreme Court, because it is a necessary element of fundamental fairness in the criminal justice system.

Key Terms

Adversarial (legal system), Bench Trial, Bill of Rights, Civil Liberties, Corrections, Courts, Crime, Criminal Justice System, Defendant, Defense Attorney, Discretion, Due Process, Due Process Clause, Equality (in Justice), Equity (in Justice), Exclusionary Rule, Fifth Amendment, Finder of Fact, Fourteenth Amendment, Incarceration, Individual Rights, Jail, Judge, Jury, Just Deserts, Justice, Lex Talionis, Parole, Police, Prison, Probation, Procedural Justice, Prosecutor, Retributive Justice, Rule of Law, Sheriff, Sheriff's Deputies, Statute, Trial by Jury, United States Code

Section 1.2: Roles, Objectives, and Limits in Criminal Justice

Learning Objectives

After Completing this section, you should be able to:

1.2(a) Describe the role of each of the three branches of government in shaping the criminal justice system.
1.2(b) Discuss the critical role of the Constitution of the United States in limiting criminal justice policy.
1.2(c) Compare and contrast the common objectives of the criminal justice system.
1.2(d) Describe the basic positions of both sides of the "Nonsystem Argument."
1.2(e) Explain the importance of rules and discretion in the operation of the criminal justice system.

Introduction

Because the criminal justice system represents a function of the "state," each of the **Three Branches of Government** has a role to play. Each branch has different responsibilities; thus, each branch depends on the other to function properly. Keep in mind that each of these three branches of government exists on the federal, state, and local level. Each of these levels of government dominates some aspect of the criminal justice system. Law enforcement is primary a local government function, as are jail operations. Making criminal laws and operating corrections agencies is primarily a state function. The federal government duplicates all criminal justice functions on a national scale. Ultimately, prisons, jails, and corrections programs can be operated at all levels of government. In practice, one level of government tends to dominate each particular function within the criminal justice system.

The Role of the Legislature

The term **legislature** refers to lawmaking assemblies such as the **Congress of the United States** or the law making bodies of all the states. Legislatures have many important functions in the criminal justice system. Perhaps the most direct function is that the legislature determines what acts are crimes and what the punishment is for particular crimes. They do this by enacting statutes. Official versions of the law that are organized by subject are called **codes**. Thus, when we refer to the **criminal code** (also called the **penal code**) we are referring to a collection of statutes that define crimes. In the **dual federalist** criminal justice system of the United States, state legislatures are the source of the bulk of criminal laws. Another crucial role of the legislature is to provide funding for criminal justice agencies and programs. Without funding, criminal justice activities would halt.

The Role of the Judiciary

The role of the **judiciary** in criminal justice is complicated by the **hierarchical** nature of the court systems. This hierarchy can be simplified by dividing courts into two major categories: **trial courts** and **appellate courts**. Trial courts adjudicate the guilt of people charged with crimes and impose sentence on those determined to be guilty. Hollywood leads to the conclusion that most criminal cases result in a trial by jury. This is substantially incorrect. The fact is that most criminal defendants who do not have their charges dropped prior to being formally charged will plead guilty. Most of those guilty pleas are a result of **plea bargaining**, an unglamorous but necessary process that takes place largely out of the public view.

Appellate courts are different in that they do not conduct criminal trials. Rather, they hear complaints raised by people who were not satisfied with their treatment by the trial court or some other aspect of the criminal justice system. The appellate courts can hear these complaints because they have the power of **judicial review**. Judicial review means that the appellate courts can review a law made by the legislature and determine if it meets constitutional standards. At the federal level, this means the standards set forth in the **Constitution** of the United States. At the state level, state appellate courts can determine if state legislatures have acted within the limits of that state's particular constitution. If the high court determines that a law is **unconstitutional**, then the law becomes void.

Appeals courts also have the power to review the actions of government employees, such as law enforcement officers and correctional officers. The most important appellate court in the United States is the **United States Supreme Court**. The day-to-day activities of police officers, for example, are heavily influenced by Supreme Court **decisions** dictating how the police must treat suspects and evidence. Keep in mind that the United States has **dual court systems** due to the structure of the American government. In a later section, the differences between the state and federal court system will be examined.

The Role of the Executive

The **executive branch** of government includes the offices of the president of the United States, governors of the fifty states, and the mayors of America's many towns and cities. Often these individuals are directly responsible for many appointments within the criminal justice system. Mayors appoint chiefs of police in many towns and cities. Governors appoint law enforcement heads as well as correctional leadership. The president appoints federal judges, including those who sit on the Supreme Court.

The executive has a key role to play in setting criminal justice agendas and galvanizing public opinion. A theme that permeates any discussion of the criminal justice system is the use and misuse of discretion. The term *discretion* is used to indicate the power that agents of the criminal justice system have to make decisions based on personal judgments. At this point in the text, the discussion centers on discretion at the highest levels of government, and how that discretion influences the criminal justice system. In later sections, the discussion will turn to how the use of discretion by officers in the field influence the operation of the system and impact the lives of citizens.

Common Objectives

The **Bureau of Justice Statistics** (1993) has identified three common goals of every element of the criminal justice system. These are efficiency, effectiveness, and fairness. **Efficiency** means economically applying available resources to accomplish statutory goals as well as to improve public safety. **Effectiveness** refers to carrying out justice system activities with proper regard for equity, proportionality, constitutional protections afforded defendants and convicted offenders, and public safety. **Fairness** refers to justice issues such as assuring equal treatment and handling of like offenders and giving equal weight to legally relevant factors in sentencing. Fairness is of such great importance because it is enshrined in the Constitution of the United States under the catchall phrase *due process*. Note that the Supreme Court has focused on **procedural due process** as the ultimate measure of justice in the United States. That is, the system of concerned with everyone being treated the same as they are processed through the system. More often than not, the fairness of individual outcomes is of little concern.

The Constitutional Framework

No matter where you live in the United States, you are protected by two independent criminal justice systems. There is always the federal system as well as the system of the state. This means that at both the state and federal level we find those who enforce the law, those who adjudicate the law, and those who punish and rehabilitate offenders. While these broad goals are the same, the particulars are quite different.

The system is further complicated by the fact that most law enforcement in the United States is done on a local level. Thus, local officers are enforcing state laws. Offenders sentenced to a period of incarceration can serve their time in local jails or state run penitentiaries. The federal system is less convoluted in that federal agents investigate federal crimes, and federal prosecutors take those cases to federal courts.

By far, state and local government takes on the largest share of the criminal justice burden. As citizens, the local police departments and sheriff's departments that serve us are whom we depend on to protect us from criminal harms.

The Nonsystem Argument

One of the most enduring debates about the criminal justice system of the United States is whether it is a **system** at all. The term *system* suggests components that work together to achieve some overarching goal. Critics argue that no such thing happens in American criminal justice. They argue that the police, courts, and corrections agencies act independently of each other with different financial resources and different goals and objectives. Many critics see a failure to organize around a central purpose, and thus we find that the criminal justice system is no system at all. This position is known as the **Nonsystem Argument**.

Rules

One common aspect of all criminal justice systems within the United States is the abundance of rules that govern criminal justice activities. These rules are hierarchical. The most important and enduring rules that must be followed by agents of the criminal justice system are those enshrined in the Constitution of the United States. Most of the safeguards of American civil liberties against intrusion by the government are contained in the Bill of Rights. The *Bill of Rights* is the first ten Amendments to the Constitution.

After the federal constitution and the constitution of the states comes federal and state statutes. The collection of federal statutes organized by topic is called the *United States Code*. States have a criminal codes as well. There are also court rules established by the high courts that bind the lower courts as well as agents of the criminal justice system. At the federal level, these are known as the *Federal Rules of Criminal Procedure*. In addition to these various laws, there are agency rules and regulations that agents of the criminal justice system must follow.

Discretion

Discretion refers to the authority the public gives agents of the criminal justice system to make decisions based on their own professional judgment. Discretion is necessary because formal rules cannot take into account every contingency criminal justice professionals encounter in practice. To function effectively, criminal justice professionals must make judgment calls. Discretion is called for when a police officer makes a decision as to whether to stop a motorist, question a suspicious person, issue a citation, make an arrest, or use deadly force. Prosecutors use discretionary powers daily in their work. Decisions must be made as to what to charge a person with, whether or not to offer a plea bargain agreement, and so forth.

Juvenile Justice

For much of history in the United States, children were treated the same as adult criminals. According to **common law**, the defense of infancy was available to children below the age of seven. The idea was that very young children were not culpable because they lacked the capacity to understand the wrongfulness of their actions. After age seven, the **infancy defense** disappeared, and children could face prison and even death. During the 19th century, society's view of children began to change. People began to realize that children were not merely miniature adults. They were still developing cognitively and morally. This new view of adolescence spawned a revolution in **juvenile justice** and led to a completely separate way of dealing with youths that committed crimes. The **Juvenile Court movement** began in the United States at the end of the Nineteenth Century. From the juvenile court statute adopted in Illinois in 1899, the system has spread to every State in the Union, the District of Columbia, and Puerto Rico.

Early reformers found the prospect of children receiving long prison sentences and sharing prison space with adult criminals appalling. There was also a conviction that the duty to children went beyond mere justice. The reformers believed that it was the duty of the state to step into the role of the parent when the parents either would not or could not correct the wayward child. Unlike adults, children were considered fundamentally good. The rigid and cold adult system was not appropriate for children; both the substantive and the procedural criminal law had to be discarded in favor of a system that fostered the best interest of the child. Thus, from inception the focus of the juvenile system was "treatment" or "rehabilitation."

Key Terms

Appellate Court, Bureau of Justice Statistics, Code, Common Law, Congress of the United States, Constitution, Criminal Code, Decisions (courts), Dual Court System, Dual Federalism, Effectiveness, Efficiency, Executive Branch, Fairness, Federal Rules of Criminal Procedure, Hierarchical, Infancy Defense, Judicial Review, Judiciary, Juvenile Court Movement, Juvenile Justice, Legislature, Nonsystem Argument, Penal Code, Plea Bargain, Procedural Due Process, System, Three Branches of Government, Trial Court, Unconstitutional, United States Supreme Court

Section 1.3: Defining and Measuring Crime

Learning Objectives

After completing this section, you should be able to:

1.3(a)   Name and describe the three major national crime data-gathering programs in the United States today.
1.3(b)   Discuss what crime statistics tell us about crime in the United States.
1.3(c)   Describe the limitations of the three major national crime data-gathering programs in the United States today.
1.3(d)   Describe the FBI's Crime Index, and list the Index Crimes.
1.3(e)   Define crime rate and explain why crime statistics are generally expressed as rates rather than counts or percentages
1.3(f)   Define the hierarchy rule and explain how it impacts crime reporting.
1.3(g)   Discuss the meaning of the term clearance rate and describe how it is different than the crime rate.
1.3(h)   Describe the development of the NIBRS, and identify why it is superior to the UCR.
1.3(i)   Compare and contrast the purpose and data collection methods of the NIBRS with the NCVS.
1.3(j)   List and define each of the Part I offenses as used in the UCR.

Introduction

A crime is an act or **omission** that is prohibited by law. For a law to be valid, a particular punishment or range of punishments must be specified. In the United States, the most common punishments are fines and imprisonment. As a matter of legal theory, a crime is a failed duty to the community for which the community will exact some punishment. This is the reason that prosecutions are always brought forward by the government, as a representation of the community that government serves. Historically, legal scholars differentiated between things that were "wrongs in themselves," which were referred to as **mala in se** offenses. These were distinct from **mala prohibita** offenses, which represented acts that were criminal merely because the government wished to prohibit them. Many criminal justice scholars use these terms to differentiate between heinous crimes like rape and murder and **victimless crimes** such as gambling and vagrancy.

Felonies, Misdemeanors, and Violations

Today, the most common and most basic division of crimes is based on the seriousness of the offense, and thus the possible punishment. **Misdemeanors** are less serious crimes that are punishable by fine and confinement in a local jail for a period not to exceed a year. **Felonies** are more serious crimes that the government punishes by fines, imprisonment (most commonly under the auspices of the state's Department of Corrections) for a period exceeding a year, or death. The distinction between misdemeanors and felonies is of ancient origin, coming to us through the **Common Law of England**. **Common law felonies** included murder, rape, mayhem, robbery, sodomy, larceny, arson, manslaughter, and burglary.

What is classified as a misdemeanor largely depends on the jurisdiction. Common examples are petty theft, prostitution, public intoxication, simple assault, disorderly conduct, and vandalism. Some crimes can be both misdemeanors and felonies, depending on the circumstances. A battery that results in a handprint on the victim's face may be classified as a misdemeanor, while a kick that breaks the victim's ribs may be a felony. Similarly, an arson that does relatively little damage (in terms of financial costs) may be a misdemeanor, while an arson that destroys a home will be a felony. These distinctions have made it into our popular culture, where criminals who commit felonies are often known as **felons**. Less commonly used is the term **misdemeanant**, who is a person convicted of misdemeanor.

Most jurisdictions recognize a class of offenses that do not result in any period of incarceration, and are punished with only a fine. These minor breaches of the law are usually called **violations**. We will delve much deeper into the particulars of what constitutes various crimes in a later section.

Measuring Crime

To understand crime and the criminal justice system, we need to understand the prevalence of crime. Good crime statistics are critically important to understanding crime trends. The more federal and state agencies know about crime trends, the more intelligently they can allocate precious resources and maximize efforts at crime suppression and prevention. Crime statistics are also frequently used as an evaluation tool for justice programs. If the **rate** of a particular crime is falling, then what the system is doing will seem to be working. If the rate of a particular crime is rising, then it will seem to indicate that the criminal justice system is failing.

In the United States, the most frequently cited crime statistics come from the FBI's **Uniform Crime Reports (UCR)**. The UCR are crime data collected by over 16,000 local and state law enforcement agencies on crimes that have been brought to the attention of police. These law enforcement agencies voluntarily send information to the FBI, which compiles them into an annual published report along with several special reports on particular issues.

Learn More Online

To learn more about the Uniform Crime Reports (UCR) and the National Incident Based Reporting System (NIBRS), visit the FBI's UCR page at:
http://www.fbi.gov/ucr/ucr.htm

Since its inception in the 1930s, many people have been critical of the UCR system for a variety of reasons. Among these reasons are the facts that the UCR includes only crimes reported to the police, only counts the most serious crime committed in a series of crimes, does not differentiate between completed crimes and attempts, and does not include many types of crimes, such as white-collar crimes and federal crimes. Another critical complaint (especially among scholars) was that the UCR did not obtain potentially important information about the victim, the offender, the location of the crime and so forth. Without this information, social scientists could not use the UCR data in attempts to explain and predict crime. These complaints eventually led to the development of a much more informative system of crime reporting known as the **National Incident Based Reporting System (NIBRS)**.

The NIBRS is an incident-based reporting system in which agencies collect data on each single crime occurrence. NIBRS data come from local, state, and federal automated records' systems. The NIBRS collects data on each single incident and arrest within 22 offense categories made up of 46 specific crimes called Group A offenses. For each of the offenses coming to the attention of law enforcement, specified types of facts about each crime are reported. In addition to the Group A offenses, there are 11 Group B offense categories for which only arrest data are reported.

According to the FBI, participating in NIBRS can benefit agencies in several ways. The benefits of participating in the NIBRS are:

- The NIBRS can furnish information on nearly every major criminal justice issue facing law enforcement today, including terrorism, white collar crime, weapons offenses, missing children where criminality is involved, drug/narcotics offenses, drug involvement in all offenses, hate crimes, spousal abuse, abuse of the elderly, child abuse, domestic violence, juvenile crime/gangs, parental abduction, organized crime, pornography/child pornography, driving under the influence, and alcohol-related offenses.

- Using the NIBRS, legislators, municipal planners/administrators, academicians, sociologists, and the public will have access to more comprehensive crime information than the summary reporting can provide.

- The NIBRS produces more detailed, accurate, and meaningful data than the traditional summary reporting. Armed with such information, law enforcement can better make a case to acquire the resources needed to fight crime.

- The NIBRS enables agencies to find similarities in crime-fighting problems so that agencies can work together to develop solutions or discover strategies for addressing the issues.

- Full participation in the NIBRS provides statistics to enable a law enforcement agency to provide a full accounting of the status of public safety within the jurisdiction to the police commissioner, police chief, sheriff, or director.

The major problem with NIBRS today is that it has not been universally implemented. Agencies and state Programs are still in the process of developing, testing, or implementing the NIBRS. In 2004, 5,271 law enforcement agencies contributed NIBRS data to the UCR Program. The data from those agencies represent 20 percent of the U.S. population and 16 percent of the crime statistics collected by the UCR Program. Implementation of NIBRS is occurring at a pace commensurate with the resources, abilities, and limitations of the contributing law enforcement agencies.

A commonly cited problem with the UCR is that there are many, many crimes that do not come to the attention of police. This problem is not limited to minor offenses. For example, it is estimated that nearly half of all rapes go unreported. These undocumented offenses are often referred to as the **dark figure of crime**. This is the reason that the United States is the Bureau of Justice Statistics' (BJS) developed the **National Crime Victimization Survey (NCVS)**. The NCVS, which began in 1973, provides a detailed picture of crime incidents, victims, and trends. Today, the survey collects detailed information on the frequency and nature of the crimes of rape, sexual assault, personal robbery, aggravated and simple assault, household burglary, theft, and motor vehicle theft. It does not measure homicide or commercial crimes (such as burglaries of stores).

Two times a year, **U.S. Census Bureau** personnel interview household members in a nationally representative sample of approximately 42,000 households (about 75,000 people). Approximately 150,000 interviews of persons age 12 or older are conducted annually. Households stay in the sample for three years. New households are rotated into the sample on an ongoing basis.

The NCVS collects information on crimes suffered by individuals and households, whether or not those crimes were reported to law enforcement. It estimates the proportion of each crime type reported to law enforcement, and it summarizes the reasons that victims give for reporting or not reporting.

The survey provides information about victims (age, sex, race, ethnicity, marital status, income, and educational level), offenders (sex, race, approximate age, and victim-offender relationship), and the crimes (time and place of occurrence, use of weapons, nature of injury, and economic consequences). Questions also cover the experiences of victims with the criminal justice system, self-protective measures used by victims, and possible substance abuse by offenders. Supplements are added periodically to the survey to obtain detailed information on topics like school crime. BJS publication of NCVS data includes Criminal

Victimization in the United States, an annual report that covers the broad range of detailed information collected by the NCVS.

Learn More Online

To learn more about the National Crime Victimization Survey (NCVS), visit the BJS Criminal Victimization page at:
http://www.ojp.usdoj.gov/bjs/cvictgen.htm

Index Crimes

The Federal Bureau of Investigation (FBI) designates certain crimes as Part I or **index offenses** because it considers them both serious and frequently reported to the police. The Part I offenses are defined as follows:

Criminal homicide: Murder and nonnegligent manslaughter: the willful (nonnegligent) killing of one human being by another. Deaths caused by negligence, attempts to kill, assaults to kill, suicides, and accidental deaths are excluded.

Forcible rape: The carnal knowledge of a female forcibly and against her will. Rapes by force and attempts or assaults to rape, regardless of the age of the victim, are included. Statutory offenses (no force used—victim under age of consent) are excluded.

Robbery: The taking or attempting to take anything of value from the care, custody, or control of a person or persons by force or threat of force or violence and/or by putting the victim in fear.

Aggravated assault: An unlawful attack by one person upon another for the purpose of inflicting severe or aggravated bodily injury. This type of assault usually is accompanied by the use of a weapon or by means likely to produce death or great bodily harm. Simple assaults are excluded.

Burglary (breaking or entering): The unlawful entry of a structure to commit a felony or a theft. Attempted forcible entry is included.

Larceny-theft (except motor vehicle theft): The unlawful taking, carrying, leading, or riding away of property from the possession or constructive possession of another. Examples are thefts of bicycles, motor vehicle parts and accessories, shoplifting, pocketpicking, or the stealing of any property or article that is not taken by force and violence or by fraud. Attempted larcenies are included. Embezzlement, confidence games, forgery, check fraud, etc., are excluded.

Motor vehicle theft: The theft or attempted theft of a motor vehicle. A motor vehicle is self-propelled and runs on land surface and not on rails. Motorboats, construction equipment, airplanes, and farming equipment are specifically excluded from this category.

Arson: Any willful or malicious burning or attempt to burn, with or without intent to defraud, a dwelling house, public building, motor vehicle or aircraft, personal property of another, etc.

Key Terms

Aggravated Assault, Arson, Burglary, Common Law Felonies, Criminal Homicide, Dark Figure of Crime, Felon, Forcible Rape, Index Offenses, Larceny-theft, Mala In Se, Mala Prohibita, Misdemeanant, Motor Vehicle Theft, National Crime Victimization Survey (NCVS), National Incident Based Reporting System (NIBRS), Omission, Rate, Robbery, U.S. Census Bureau, Uniform Crime Reports (UCR), Victimless Crime, Violation

Section 1.4: The Criminal Justice Process

Learning Objectives

After completing this section, you should be able to:

1.4(a) Define the vocabulary related to criminal case processing.
1.4(b) Explain the basic legal requirements for a lawful arrest.
1.4(c) Describe the tasks involved in the booking process.
1.4(d) Describe the two major types of charging documents.
1.4(e) Describe the purpose of an initial appearance.
1.4(f) Describe the role of the preliminary hearing and the grand jury.
1.4(g) Describe the tasks involved in an arraignment.

Introduction

As we pointed out in the previous section, crimes often do not come to the attention of law enforcement. This is what is called the *dark figure of crime*. The criminal justice process does not begin until crimes come to the attention of police. Since many crimes go unreported, a majority of crimes never begin the process. Those that do generally enter the system from the private sector. That is, most criminal prosecutions begin with a private citizen making a report to police. Very few offenses are detected by officers performing random patrols, contrary to the conventional wisdom that preventive patrol serves to prevent crime. Information from private citizens is the key to success in the criminal justice system.

Investigation

Once a crime is reported to the police, an investigation will begin. Depending on the nature and seriousness of the crime, this investigation may be as simple as a patrol officer asking a few questions at the scene, or as complex as involving detectives and forensic scientists. The first responder will conduct a preliminary investigation. The **preliminary investigation** involves securing the crime scene and identifying victims, perpetrators, and witnesses. Other tasks that do not involve specialized training and large amounts of time are also part of the preliminary investigation. Cases that are more complex will require a **follow-up investigation**, which is usually conducted by a detective.

Arrest

An **arrest** involves taking a person into actual physical custody by law enforcement. For an arrest to be legal, it must be based on **probable cause**. Probable cause means that enough evidence is present to convince a reasonable person that it is more likely than not that the suspect committed the crime. Perhaps one of the most controversial aspects of the arrest process is the use of force by police in making an arrest. Constitutional and statutory law authorizes the use of *reasonable* force when the force is necessary to take a suspect into custody. Often, what constitutes **reasonable force** is a hotly disputed matter. In the landmark case of ***Graham v. Connor*** (1989), the Supreme Court of the United States established the legal requirement that the use of force by police be **objectively reasonable**. This standard suggests that police may use an amount of force that a reasonable person would conclude was necessary to effect the arrest and no more. Note that the force used to effect an arrest is a different legal issue than self-defense. Officers are always allowed to answer deadly force with deadly force when lives are at stake.

Booking

After an arrest, suspects are taken to a police station holding facility or jail for **booking**. The difference depends largely on the size of the jurisdiction. Large municipal agencies often have their own holding cells, while small and rural agencies usually use the county jail for booking and holding purposes. Booking is the process of officially recording that a person has been arrested. This usually involves identifying, photographing, and fingerprinting the suspect. The identification process usually involves recording the suspect's personal information, such as their legal name, date of birth, address, physical characteristics, and so forth. Most jails will have a standardized booking form for this purpose. An official record is also made at this time about the alleged crime committed by the suspect. The suspect's identifying information will usually be retrieved from a criminal history database. The suspect will also be photographed and fingerprinted. These identification tasks have been made swift and accurate by modern digital technologies. The suspect will be thoroughly searched for contraband, and all personal property will be confiscated and inventoried. The property is returned to the suspect upon release unless it is deemed illegal contraband or evidence of a crime. Note that in most jurisdictions, persons suspected of minor offenses can be issued a written citation in lieu of being booked into jail. By signing the citation, the person is promising to appear in court at the date and time listed on the citation.

Charging

This crucial step is where law enforcement and prosecutors make the decision as to what particular crime to charge a suspect with, if at all. The usual process is for police to turn over a case file to the prosecutor's office. The case file will contain the police **arrest report**, along with supporting documentation such as witness statements, victims statements, forensic laboratory reports, and so on. The prosecutor will determine if there is enough evidence to go forward with the case. If there appears to be enough evidence to go forward in the prosecutor's professional legal judgment, then a **charging document** is filed with the court. The name of the charging document changes from jurisdiction to jurisdiction. Some jurisdictions (including the federal courts) require an **indictment** by a grand jury, and others use a prosecutorial **information**. Note that an arrest does not always precede the issuance of a charging document. There are times when the charging document is filed first, and then a warrant is issued for the arrest of the accused. This situation is most common in jurisdictions where grand jury indictments are a common charging document.

Initial Appearance

Under the constitution, people cannot be seized and jailed without reasonable cause. To make sure that no one is arrested and held illegally, every arrestee has the right to be brought before a judge within hours of arrest. During this first or **initial appearance**, a **magistrate** will inform the suspect of the charges against him, advise him of his rights, and determine if there is enough evidence to hold the suspect for further processing. These hearings tend to be less formal than later formal hearings, and can be conducted by lower court magistrates who may or may not have the authority to preside over the actual criminal trial. In most jurisdictions, bail is set at this stage in the process.

At the federal level, the process is somewhat formalized, and several important tasks are taken care of in this single step. At an initial appearance in federal court, a judge advises the defendant of the charges filed, considers whether the defendant should be held in jail until trial, and determines whether there is probable cause to believe that an offense has been committed, and the defendant has committed it. Defendants who are unable to afford **counsel** are advised of their right to a court-appointed attorney. The court may appoint either a federal public defender or a private attorney who has agreed to accept such appointments from the court. Regardless of the type of appointment, the attorney will be paid by the court from funds appropriated by Congress. Defendants released into the community before trial may be required to obey certain restrictions, such as home confinement or drug testing, and to make periodic reports to a **pretrial services officer** to ensure appearance at trial.

Preliminary Hearing and the Grand Jury

As a matter of American legal tradition, a **grand jury** was convened to hear evidence presented by the prosecutor and determine if that evidence was sufficient to warrant a full-blown criminal trial. In other words, it was the duty of the grand jury to determine if probable cause existed in a particular criminal case. Defendants had no right to be present at grand jury proceedings, and these deliberations were held in secret.

States that were more populous found that the grand jury system was unwieldy. It was too labor intensive and took up too much time. These states developed a system whereby the prosecutor files a charging document called an **information** with the court. A hearing is then held to determine if probable cause is indeed present as the prosecution alleges. Defendants have the right to be present at these **preliminary hearings**. Regardless of whether a grand jury system us used or prosecutorial information is used, the gold standard for moving forward to a criminal trial is probable cause.

The federal courts still use the old grand jury system. At the beginning of a federal criminal case, the principal actors are the **U.S. Attorney** (the prosecutor) and the grand jury. The U.S. attorney represents the United States in most court proceedings, including all criminal prosecutions. The grand jury reviews evidence presented by the U.S. attorney and decides whether there is sufficient evidence to require a defendant to stand trial.

Arraignment

At this stage, the criminal defendant appears in court to have the formal charging document read. This is where the defendant enters a **plea**. The most common pleas are guilty and not guilty. In most jurisdictions, **standing mute** (saying nothing when asked for a plea) will result in the court entering a not guilty plea on behalf of the defendant. If a defendant pleads guilty in return for the government agreeing to drop certain charges or to recommend a lenient sentence, the agreement often is called a **plea bargain**.

In federal criminal courts, the defendant enters a plea to the charges brought by the U.S. attorney. More than 90% of federal criminal defendants plead guilty rather than go to trial. If the defendant pleads guilty, the judge may impose a sentence at that time, but more commonly will schedule a hearing to determine the sentence at a later date. In most felony cases, the judge waits for the results of a **presentence report**, prepared by the court's probation office, before imposing sentence. If the defendant pleads not guilty, the judge will proceed to schedule a trial.

Because of the seriousness of a guilty plea, the judge must determine that a guilty plea was made both **knowingly and voluntarily**. If it is determined that a guilty plea is entered knowingly and voluntarily, there is no need to go on with a trial. In many cases, the judge will impose a sentence at this point.

The Sequence of Events in the Criminal Justice System

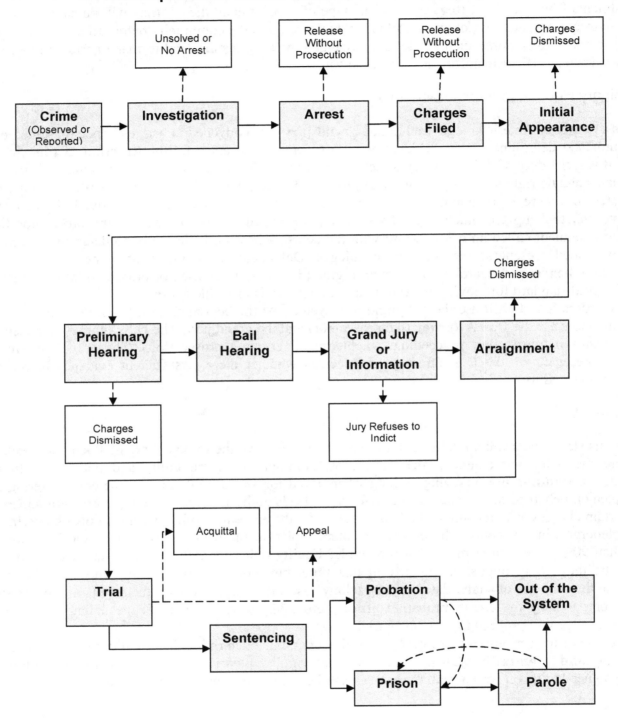

Key Terms

Arrest, Arrest Report, Booking, Charging Document, Counsel, Follow Up Investigation, Graham v. Connor (1989), Grand Jury, Indictment, Information, Initial Appearance, Knowingly and Voluntarily, Magistrate, Objectively Reasonable, Plea, Preliminary Hearing, Preliminary Investigation, Presentence Report, Pretrial Services Officer, Probable Cause, Reasonable Force, Standing Mute, U.S. Attorney

Section 1.5: The Criminal Justice Process (Continued)

Learning Objectives

After completing this section, you should be able to:

1.5(a)   List and describe the various steps on the criminal justice process.
1.5(b)   Describe how discretionary decisions impact case flow through the criminal justice system.
1.5(c)   Define bail and describe when bail may be denied to an accused person.
1.5(d)   Differentiate between a jury trial and a bench trial.
1.5(e)   Explain why criminal trials are said to be an adversarial process.
1.5(f)   List and define the various criminal sentences commonly used in the United States today.
1.5(g)   Outline the appeals process, describing the duties of each actor in the process.
1.5(h)   Explain how the criminal justice process can be compared to a "funnel."

Pretrial Detention or Bail

Pretrial detention refers to keeping the suspect in jail until trial. Most criminal suspects are released on **bail** prior to trial. Bail is a specified amount of money paid by the defendant to ensure that they will show up in court on the appointed day. If they do not show up, the bail is forfeited and a **bench warrant** is issued for the person's arrest. The right to bail is not a constitutional guarantee as many think. The actual constitutional rule is that excessive bail may not be required. If an accused person is determined by the courts to be a flight risk, then the judge may deny bail and hold the person in jail until trial. Such a period of incarceration prior to trial is known as **pretrial detention**.

Plea Bargaining

A **plea bargain** is a negotiated agreement between the prosecution and the defendant. In most cases, the defendant agrees to plead guilty to a lesser crime than that originally charged, or to a lesser sentence than can normally be expected if the case goes to trial. There are many critics of the plea bargaining process, but it is unavoidable in our criminal justice system.

Trial

The purpose of a **trial** is to answer the basic question of the defendant's guilt. A finding of guilt must be based on facts (evidence), and accordingly the persons reaching this decision are referred to in legal documents and texts as the "finders of fact." This can be a jury in a jury trial, or a judge acting alone in what is referred to as a **bench trial**. Recall that the American legal system is adversarial, which means that two sides must contest the issue of guilt in court. The prosecution attempts to prove the guilt of the defendant, and the defense attempts to demonstrate the accused person's innocence. As a technical matter, the burden of proof is on the state (prosecution). This legal jargon means that the defendant does not have to do anything at all; it is up to the prosecutor to prove guilt. As a practical matter, doing nothing is rarely employed as a defense strategy. In a criminal trial, guilt must be proven **beyond a reasonable doubt (BRD)**. This is a very high **evidentiary standards**—the highest known to our legal system.

Sentencing

If the defendant pleads guilty or is found guilty, a judge (or jury in some states) will hand down a **sentence**. Possible sentences include **monetary fines**, probation, periods of incarceration in jail or prison, or some combination of supervision and incarceration.

At the federal level, the judge determines the defendant's sentence according to special federal **sentencing guidelines** issued by the **United States Sentencing Commission**. The court's probation office prepares a report for the court that applies the sentencing guidelines to the individual defendant and the crimes for which he or she is guilty. During sentencing, the court may consider not only the evidence produced at trial, but all relevant information that may be provided by the pretrial services officer, the U.S. attorney, and the defense attorney. In unusual circumstances, the court may depart from the sentence calculated according to the sentencing guidelines. The federal sentencing guidelines have been controversial, and have resulted in a huge number of appeals court cases where the person being sentenced disagreed with the guidelines or their application.

A federal court's sentence may include time in prison, a fine to be paid to the government, and **restitution** to be paid to crime victims. The court's **probation officers** assist the court in enforcing any conditions that are imposed as part of a criminal sentence. The supervision of offenders also may involve services such as substance abuse testing and treatment programs, job counseling, and alternative detention options.

Appeal

The decisions of trial courts are not set in stone. If some legal rule is violated, the convict can **appeal** the decision to a higher court in an effort to have the wrong corrected. A successful appeal usually means that the trial court is ordered to rehear the case while fixing the problem that the appeals court found with the first trial. Of course, a rehearing of the case by the trial court is not mandatory. If the prosecutor believes that the state cannot prove guilt beyond a reasonable doubt given the appellate court's directions, then the case will be dropped.

The losing party in a decision by a trial court in the federal system normally is entitled to appeal the decision to a federal court of appeals. In criminal cases, the defendant may appeal a guilty verdict, but the government may not appeal if a defendant is found not guilty. Either side in a criminal case may appeal with respect to the sentence that is imposed after a guilty verdict.

The party to a case who files an appeal is known as an **appellant**. The appellant must show that the trial court (or sometimes an administrative agency) made a legal error that affected the decision in the case. The court of appeals makes its decision based on the record of the case established by the trial court. It does not receive additional evidence or hear witnesses. The court of appeals also may review the factual findings of the trial court or agency, but typically may only overturn a decision on factual grounds if the findings were "clearly erroneous."

In appeals heard by the **United States Circuit Courts**, panels of three judges working together decide cases. The appellant presents legal arguments to the panel, in writing, in a document called a **brief**. In the brief, the appellant tries to persuade the judges that the trial court made an error, and that its decision should be reversed. On the other hand, the party defending against the appeal, known as the **appellee**, tries in its brief to show why the trial court decision was correct, or why any error made by the trial court was not significant enough to affect the outcome of the case.

Although some cases are decided on the basis of written briefs alone, many cases are selected for an **oral argument** before the court. Oral argument in the court of appeals is a structured discussion between the appellate lawyers and the panel of judges focusing on the legal principles in dispute. Each side is given a short time (usually about 15 minutes) to present arguments to the court. The court of appeals decision usually will be the final word in the case, unless it sends the case back to the trial court for additional proceedings, or the parties ask the U.S. Supreme Court to review the case. In some cases the decision may be reviewed *en banc*, that is, by a larger group of judges (usually all) of the court of appeals for the circuit.

A litigant who loses in a federal court of appeals, or in the highest court of a state, may file a petition for a *writ of certiorari*, which is a document asking the Supreme Court to review the case. The Supreme Court, however, does not have to grant review. The Court typically will agree to hear a case only when it involves an unusually important legal principle, or when two or more federal appellate courts have interpreted a law differently. There are also a small number of special circumstances in which the Supreme Court is required by law to hear an appeal. When the Supreme Court hears a case, the parties are required to file written briefs and the Court may hear oral argument.

Corrections

Corrections is designed to protect the public and serve the public interest by punishing or rehabilitating criminal offenders, depending on one's philosophy. The idea of corrections is much broader that just prisons and jails where convicts serve out entire sentences. It also encompasses mechanisms of early release, such as probation and parole. The corrections system in the United States is immense. On any given day, about 7 million Americans are under some sort of correctional supervision. Although only about a third of convicted offenders are actually incarcerated, the number of convicts in America's prisons is quite large. This translates into massive public expenditures. Because it is so expensive, corrections remains a topic of much political debate.

Release from the System

The final state of the criminal justice process is release from the system. If an offender is released from confinement on parole, then the conditions of parole must be met and severe limitations are placed on the offender. Offenders that have served a complete prison sentenced and "**flat timed**," are free of parole conditions and can return to a semblance of life before entry into the criminal justice system.

The Criminal Justice Funnel

The criminal justice system is frequently described as acting much like a funnel. Just as the funnel is wide at the top and narrow at the bottom, so too is the criminal justice system. That is to say, as we move forward in the criminal justice process, we find fewer and fewer cases. At every step along the way, people drop out of the system. Of all the crimes known to police, very few result in convictions and prison sentences. The police may decide to deal with a case informally. Prosecutors may decide not to prosecute a case. Judges may decide on treatment rather than imprisonment. These are just a few examples of people leaving the system prior to incarceration.

Decision Points in the Criminal Justice Process			
Decision Maker	**Task**	**Decision to move forward...**	**Decision to Stop...**
Complainant	Inform police.	Police are informed.	Nothing is done.
Police	Investigation.	An arrest is made.	No arrest is made.
Prosecutor	Charging.	Charges are filed with the court.	No charges are filed.
Judge	Initial Appearance.	Defendant is held over for trial.	Defendant is released.
Defendant	Plead.	Plead not guilty.	Plead guilty.
Jury	Decide guilt.	Find the defendant guilty.	Find the defendant not guilty.
Judge or Jury (Depending on jurisdiction)	Determine sentence.	Sentence offender to incarceration.	Sentence the offender to community supervision.

Key Terms

Appeal, Appellant, Bail, Bench Warrant, Beyond a Reasonable Doubt (BRD), Burden of Proof, Criminal Justice Funnel, *En Banc*, **Evidentiary Standard, Flat Timed, Monetary Fine, Oral Argument, Petition for a** *Writ of Certiorari*, **Pretrial Detention, Probation Officer, Restitution, Sentence, Sentencing Guidelines, Trial, United States Circuit Courts, United States Sentencing Commission**

Chapter 2: The Political and Legal Environment

The criminal justice system is bounded and controlled by law. Both the law and the functioning of the criminal justice system are highly political in nature. For this reason, understanding the influence of these two interrelated factors is critical to understanding the functioning of the criminal justice system. Of particular importance is the political artifact of **dual federalism**. Dual federalism refers to the political system in the United States where power is split between the federal and state governments, and to a lesser extent, local governments.

Section 2.1: Dual Federalism

Learning Objectives

After Completing this section, you should be able to:

2.1(a)   Describe the dual court system of the United States.
2.1(b)   Explain the role of federal courts in dealing with state cases.
2.1(c)   Explain the checks and balances that curtail the power of the courts.
2.1(d)   Explain the analogies of "layer cake" and "marble cake" used to describe federalism in the United States today.
2.1(e)   Explain the role of local governments in the criminal justice system.

Introduction

Dual federalism refers to the governmental system of the United States where there are 50 state governments and a single federal government. At least theoretically, the states are allowed to exercise their own powers without interference from the federal government. In other words, some powers are delegated to the federal government while others remain with the states. In reality, this boils down to an ever-evolving body of law. The trend has been toward the federal government gaining more and more influence in the sphere of criminal justice over the years since the Constitution was drafted.

The Hierarchy of Laws

Article Six of the U.S. Constitution has long been interpreted as meaning that federal law trumps state law whenever the two come into conflict. Conversely, the power of the federal government was thought to be held in check by the **Bill of Rights**, which is the first ten amendments to the Constitution. The exact reach of federal power has long been debated and is still not fully resolved. Major changes in how the federal government exercised its power in relation to the states have happened quickly at times, such as a dramatic increase in federal power during the Civil War, the passage of the Fourteenth Amendment immediately after the war, and during the New Deal era prior to World War II. Many political scientists contend that dual federalism is no longer an accurate term, stating that the states and the federal government share powers in a model that may more accurately be described as **cooperative federalism**. Nowhere has this overlap of power been more obvious than in the criminal laws of the United States and how those laws overlap the criminal codes of the various states.

The Hierarchy of Courts

As a direct result of American federalism, a dual court system exists within the United States today. There is a complete and independent federal court system, and there is a complete and somewhat independent state court system in every state. The idea of **separation of powers** does not suggest that the courts are completely independent of the other branches of government. The laws that federal courts arbitrate, for example, are passed by Congress and signed by the President. The federal courts, in turn, have the authority to decide the constitutionality of federal laws and resolve other disputes over them. On the other hand, judges depend upon the executive branch to enforce court decisions. It can be seen from these few examples that the branches of government depend on each other to function.

The U.S. Constitution gives Congress the power to create federal courts other than the Supreme Court and to determine the jurisdiction of those courts. It is Congress, not the judges, that controls the type of cases that may be addressed in the various federal courts. Congress has other constitutional responsibilities that determine how the courts operate. Congress decides how many judges there should be and where they will work. Congress, through the confirmation process, has a role in determining which presidential nominees eventually become federal judges. Congress also approves the federal courts' budget and appropriates money for the judiciary to operate (Congress wields this authority over many components of the criminal justice system. The power to control funding is often called the **power of the purse**). According to the Administrative Office of the US Courts, "the judiciary's budget is a very small part—substantially less than one percent—of the entire federal budget."

United States District Courts

The **United States District Courts** are the trial courts of the federal court system. Within limits set by Congress and the Constitution, the district courts have jurisdiction to hear nearly all categories of federal cases, including both civil and criminal matters. There are 94 federal judicial districts, including at least one district in each state, the District of Columbia and Puerto Rico. Three territories of the United States—the Virgin Islands, Guam, and the Northern Mariana Islands—have district courts that hear federal cases.

United States Courts of Appeal

The 94 U.S. judicial districts are organized into 12 regional circuits, each of which has a **United States Court of Appeals**. A court of appeals hears appeals from the district courts located within its circuit, as well as appeals from decisions of federal administrative agencies. Because these courts are organized into circuits, they are sometimes referred to as **circuit courts**.

The United States Supreme Court (USSC)

The United States Supreme Court consists of the Chief Justice of the United States and eight associate justices. At its discretion, and within certain guidelines established by Congress, the Supreme Court each year hears a limited number of the cases it is asked to decide. Those cases may begin in the federal or state courts, and they usually involve important questions about the Constitution or federal law. This standard is often referred to as a **substantial federal question**. Thus, only certain state court cases are eligible for review by the U.S. Supreme Court. State courts are the final deciders of state laws and constitutions. Their interpretations of federal law or the U.S. Constitution may be appealed to the U.S. Supreme Court. The Supreme Court may choose to hear or not to hear such cases.

State Court Structures

The Constitution and laws of each state establish the state courts. A **court of last resort**, often known as a supreme court, is usually the highest court in a state. Some states also have an **intermediate court of appeals**. Below these appeals courts are the state trial courts. Some are referred to as circuit or district courts. Historically, states usually had courts that handled specific legal matters, (e.g., probate courts, juvenile court, family court, etc.). Many states, however, have followed the federal model and have combined these various courts. Parties dissatisfied with the decision of the trial court may take their cases to the intermediate court of appeals in states that have them, or to the court of last resort in states that do not.

The Hierarchy of Lawmakers

As previously discussed, Article Six of the United States Constitution contains what is known as the **supremacy clause**. The second clause of Article VI of the Constitution of the United States pronounces: "This Constitution, and the Laws of the United States which shall be made in Pursuance thereof; and all Treaties made, or which shall be made, under the Authority of the United States, shall be the supreme Law of the Land; and the Judges in every State shall be bound thereby; any Thing in the Constitution or Laws of any State to the Contrary notwithstanding." What exactly this means has been subject to interpretation over the years, but several Supreme Court cases have clarified things.

In *Gibbons v. Ogden* (1824), for example, the court stated that when laws "though enacted in the execution of acknowledged State powers, interfere with, or are contrary to the laws of Congress, made in pursuance of the Constitution…the act of Congress…is supreme; and the law of the State, though enacted in the exercise of powers not controverted, must yield to it." This means that when a federal law (so long as it is constitutional) comes into conflict with a state law, the federal law wins and the state law is null and void.

The Dual Executive

Often neglected in discussions of federalism are the issues that arise from having dual executive functions within the government structures of the states as well as the federal government. Just as there are federal laws and federal courts, there are federal law enforcement agencies. The federal agencies can only enforce federal laws. Law enforcement officers within those states only enforce state laws. Importantly, each level of government can provide support for the law enforcement efforts of the other.

The Third Layer of Cake

The dual federalist system in the United States has been referred to (especially in its earlier versions) as **layer cake federalism**. The idea of a layer cake suggests the distinct yet united spheres of power held by the federal government and by the various states. In a 1960 report entitled *Goals for Americans: The Report of the President's Commission on National Goals*, political scientist Morton Grodzins compared the layer cake analogy to **marble cake federalism**. The marbling of this type of cake symbolized the overlapping and concurring powers of the state and federal governments.

Often forgotten in this power tug of war between the state and federal governments is that there is a third tier of government within nearly every jurisdiction in the United States: the local governments. The term **local government** is used to discuss the governing bodies of America's myriad cities and counties. Local governments are critically important to criminal justice because most of the workload of the criminal justice system is taken care of on a local level. The vast majority of police officers are employed at the municipal (city) level of government. A large number of law enforcement officers and correctional officers are employed by county (or parish, depending on the state) governments under the auspices of the Sheriff's Department.

For legal purposes, most local and county agencies are considered state agencies. Municipal police officers and county deputies are charged with enforcing state laws; they can do nothing about violations of federal law except for turning a case over to federal authorities. Local governments are also empowered to make "minor" laws known as ordinances. In the criminal justice system, ordinances regulating conduct are usually considered violations, resulting in only a fine. Local governments are not entrusted by the state and federal governments with the power to enact laws that punish by imprisonment.

Key Terms

Article Six, Circuit Courts, Cooperative Federalism, Court of Last Resort, *Gibbons v. Ogden* **(1824), Intermediate Court of Appeals, Layer Cake Federalism, Local Government, Marble Cake Federalism, Power of the Purse, Separation of Powers, Substantial Federal Question, Supremacy Clause, United States Courts of Appeals, United States District Courts**

Section 2.2: Politics in Criminal Justice

Learning Objectives

After completing this section, you should be able to:

2.2(a) Describe the impact of executive branch politics on the criminal justice system.

2.2(b) Describe the role of legislative branch politics in shaping criminal justice policy.

2.2(c) Describe the impact of local and state politics on policing.

2.2(d) Explain Herbert Packer's crime control model and due process model, giving examples of policies that would fit each.

2.2(e) Trace the development of the juvenile justice system within the United States.

Introduction

Politics is the art and science of running a government and guiding governmental policy. The nature of politics in America is conflict and debate about policy, and criminal justice policy falls into that arena. The American political system and the criminal justice system involve actions of the President, Congers, courts, bureaucracies, interest groups, elections, and the media. These groups are mirrored on the state level and to some degree on the local level. The actions of elected officials have a direct impact on the system, and the policies they implement directly affect how justice is done.

The Politics of Selecting Decision Makers

In a democratic republic, one of two ways selects criminal justice decision makers: They either are elected by the public, or are appointed by a public official (often an elected one). Elected mayors, for example, often appoint chiefs of police. The President of the United States (an elected official) appoints Supreme Court justices with the confirmation of the U.S. Senate (a body of elected officials). Both methods are highly political and cannot be understood without understanding something of the political process.

The Politics of Lawmaking

Although the federal legal system and that of most states rely on the old common law for their historical foundations, criminal law is mostly a matter of statute these days. That is, criminal laws are made by legislative assemblies that decide which acts are prohibited, and what punishments are appropriate for those that commit those acts in violation of the law. Obviously, politics influences the laws that assemblies pass. Today the nation finds itself at the conclusion of what has been a "get tough" era of criminal justice. Ushered in by the "crack epidemic" of the early 1980s, this has been a period of harsher punishments, longer prison sentences, less therapeutic programs, and skyrocketing corrections budgets. The pendulum seems to have reached the far right, and now may be swinging back toward the middle. Many states have begun concentrated efforts at finding alternatives to incarceration, and the federal government is considering early release for drug offenders sentenced under the "get tough" drug laws of the previous two decades.

The Politics of Policing

Most police departments try to distance themselves from the vicissitudes of politics as much as possible. To be effective, law enforcement must be seen as fair and impartial, serving all of the community without favoritism or political patronage. The political climate of a community can have a huge impact on the police department. Elected officials appoint police administrators, and can often fire them just as easily. The style of law enforcement, formal departmental policy, and informal norms can all be heavily influenced by local politics. The structure of local government can have an impact on how police services are delivered. Professional city managers, for example, are less likely to get involved in police affairs than are mayors and city council members.

The Politics of Prosecution

While police departments are often somewhat shielded from politics and influenced by it indirectly, prosecutors in most jurisdictions are elected officials and thus highly political. At the federal level, an essentially political process appoints U.S. attorneys. The career paths of these federal lawyers tend to be linked to one particular political party or the other. It is common to see prosecutors at both the state and federal level using their tenure as prosecutors to launch political careers. This fact gives rise to the unethical possibility of political prosecutions against political enemies. In fact, many at the time stated that this was the sort of thing that was happening with the impeachment proceedings launched against then-President Bill Clinton.

The Politics of the Judiciary

There is a tendency among academic writers to view the judiciary as somehow above partisan politics. In the modern American reality, this is a pleasant fiction. Judges at all levels of government are either elected or appointed, and this fact makes them political creatures. Elected judges fear public reactions to issues with political foundations, such as appearing "soft on crime" or being in favor of the death penalty, or for it, depending on the political climate in the judge's jurisdiction. Those political affiliations and beliefs necessarily inform judges' decisions. Conservative courts tend to side with law and order, willing to sacrifice some civil liberties to maintain law and order. Liberal judges tend to take the opposite, ruling in favor of civil liberties at the expense of (in the minds of the opposition) public safety. It has been said that the real job of appellate courts is balancing the civil rights of the people with the desire of the people to be safe from crime. Obviously, the political beliefs of the justices making these decisions weighs heavily in the outcome of important cases.

The Politics of Corrections

As with the other elements of the criminal justice systems, corrections is a highly politicized aspect of government. At the local level, the operation of jails is tied to the office of sheriff in many jurisdictions, which ties jail operations to the politics of particular individuals being elected and reelected as sheriff. At the state level, departments of corrections are highly political, with administrators and budgets being politically determined. Another highly political aspect of corrections is the membership and functioning of parole boards, which is established by appointment of the governor in most jurisdictions. If parole boards make release decisions that later reflect badly on the board members, the bad press will ultimately turn to the governor.

The Politicization of Justice

As politics is such an integral part of criminal justice, a high potential for serious problems generated by politics exists. Rash decisions can be made, poorly considered policies can be implemented, and ill-conceived laws can be written that hamper the efficient and ethical administration of justice. Unscrupulous politicians can easily make appeals to people's emotions, fears, and prejudices to improve their own chances at reappointment or reelection. Sadly, emotionally charged decisions do not tend to be rational decisions. In the high-stakes world of criminal justice, clear, rational thinking is often overshadowed by politically charged emotionality.

Crime Control versus Due Process

Herbert Packer (1964) outlined two competing models of the value systems operating within criminal justice today: The **crime control model** and the **due process model**. These two models of how the justice system should operate reflect two opposing sets of political ideologies that have a massive impact on criminal justice decision-making at all levels. The divide is not as simple as Democrat or Republican. Both models represent core values in the American way of life. After all, every good citizen wants to see crime controlled. We want to live in safe, orderly communities. As Americans, we also highly value freedom. We loath the idea of oppressive governments that interfere with our personal liberties. We are proud of our rights to be free from government oppression, and we value our right to privacy.

According to Packer, "The value system that underlies the Crime Control Model is based on the proposition that the repression of criminal conduct is by far the most important function to be performed by the criminal process." There is a definite political philosophy that underlies this assertion: "The failure of law enforcement to bring criminal conduct under tight control is viewed as leading to the breakdown of public order and thence to the disappearance of an important condition of human freedom. If the laws go unenforced, which is to say, if it is perceived that there is a high percentage of failure to apprehend and convict in the criminal process, a general disregard for legal controls tends to develop." Therefore, adherents of the Crime Control Model advocate enhancing the powers of the police to investigate and prosecute criminals. These necessarily include enhanced powers of search and seizure. Under this philosophy of criminal justice, the primary focus of the system should be discovering the truth and establishing the facts.

The Due Process Model takes a rather opposite view of how the system should operate. The key to understanding this position is that it hinges on protecting the civil rights of every citizen. Under this philosophy, the most important function of the criminal justice system is to ensure procedural due process, which mean maintaining fundamental fairness in all aspects of the criminal justice process. A major policy implication if this view is to limit police powers in order to prevent the oppression of the individual citizen. Adherents of this position hold that merely establishing guilt is not adequate; the government must show guilt in a fair and legal way that respects the rights of the accused.

In reality, the courts and other elements of the criminal justice system have to strike a balance of these two positions. It must be realized that the relative importance of each of these positions is not static: There is a constant tug of war between the two positions. As the makeup of America's high courts change, so too does the underlying philosophy that dominates the decisions of those courts. Liberal courts establish broad civil liberties, and conservative courts erode those liberties in the name of law and order.

The Juvenile Justice System

The 1800s saw a revolution in the way Americans controlled juvenile delinquency. The movement away from treating juveniles as adults began as early as 1825 when the Society for the Prevention of Juvenile Delinquency began advocating separate facilities for juvenile offenders. Privately run juvenile facilities sprang up, and soon generated controversy over reported abuses. This criticism led many states to create their own juvenile detention facilities.

Detention facilities were not the only facet of the system that was changing. Illinois passed the **Juvenile Court Act of 1899**, which established the America's first juvenile court. The British policy of **parens patriae** (the government as the parent) was the rationale for the state becoming involved in the lives of children differently than it did with adult offenders. The doctrine was interpreted to mean that the state had both the right and the obligation to intervene when natural parents failed to discipline adequately and protect children. A critical aspect of the developing juvenile justice system was a focus on the welfare of the child. Delinquent youths were seen as being in need of the benevolent guidance of the court. Rather than merely punishing delinquents for their wrongdoings, juvenile courts sought to turn delinquents into productive citizens through treatment rather than the punitive measures used in adult cases.

By 1910, 32 States had established juvenile courts, and many of those had established probation services. By 1925, all but two States had established the foundations of a juvenile justice system. The statutes that created these courts made the doctrine of *parens patriae* explicit. The different philosophy of the juvenile courts led to both substantive and procedural differences between adult cases and juvenile cases. Ultimately, most states had systems where those accused of crimes and less than 18 years of age had their cases heard in juvenile courts. An important difference was that juvenile courts were not adversarial in nature, and prosecutors were not responsible for bringing cases before the court. Juvenile courts tended to handle their own intake. Juvenile courts were prone to consider extralegal factors when deciding how to deal with a particular case. Many juvenile courts had intake procedures that allowed for the informal diversion of youthful offenders where no formal judicial action was taken.

Another major difference between juvenile courts and adult courts was the level of formality. Juvenile proceedings were handled in a much less formal way than adult trials. Because the court used the **best interest of the child** standard, many due process protections afforded adult defendants were considered unnecessary. A wide range of dispositions was available for juvenile judges seeking to rehabilitate wayward children. The doctrine of proportionality did not necessarily apply, and delinquent children could receive anything from a verbal warning to being locked up in a secure detention facility. The duration of these dispositions was very fluid. The child would continue his or her "treatment" until they were cured, or became an adult.

By the 1960s, many people had become disillusioned with the juvenile courts and their ability to rehabilitate. The treatment options available to juvenile judges never achieved the level of success that the public demanded. The underlying assumptions about the validity of individualized treatment of delinquent youths were not widely challenged, but the application of the philosophy by the juvenile courts was brought into question.

The 1960s saw a radical change in society and the United States Supreme Court's opinions regarding civil liberties. These changes, while causing radical changes in police procedure, were also felt by the juvenile justice system. The justices believed that children should be afforded many of the same constitutional safeguards to their liberty as adult offenders. Accordingly, they made several rulings in a short span of time that protected these rights. A side effect of these procedural protections was the formalization of the juvenile courts. Juvenile courts started to look much more like adult courts than they did at their inception. Delinquents facing the possibility of confinement were guaranteed the right to an attorney, protection against self-incrimination, and the right to receive notice of the charges. The standard of proof changed from a **preponderance of the evidence** to beyond a reasonable doubt in juvenile cases.

The Supreme Court declined to extend all adult rights to children. They, for example, determined that juveniles had no right to a trial by jury. Congress was not silent on juvenile justice issues during this time. In the **Juvenile Delinquency Prevention and Control Act of 1968**, Congress recommended that children charged with nonserious status offenses be handled outside the court system. This was the beginning of a movement toward community-based sanctions, **deinstitutionalization**, and moving juvenile offenders away from adult offenders.

The "get tough on crime" movement that swept the Nation during the 1980s did not leave the juvenile justice system unscathed. The public perception was that serious juvenile crime was on the rise, and that the juvenile courts were too lenient on offenders. Many states responded to this public outcry for tougher sanctions by passing laws that are more punitive. One of the most controversial strategies was the removal of certain classes of offenders from the juvenile system and placing them in the adult system. Others revamped their juvenile courts to operate more like adult courts. As a result, offenders charged with certain offenses are excluded from juvenile court jurisdiction or face mandatory **waiver** to criminal court. Prior to this time, a waiver to adult courts was possible, but it was relatively rare and done on a case-by-case basis.

Every state made modifications to the juvenile justice system during the 1990s. These were widely varied. Three major components were changed in nearly every state. State legislatures passed laws that made it easier to transfer juveniles from the juvenile justice system to the criminal justice system. Most states passed laws that gave criminal and juvenile courts expanded sentencing options. Most legislatures also modified or removed traditional juvenile court confidentiality provisions by making records and proceedings more open to the public.

Key Terms

Best Interest of the Child, Crime Control Model, Deinstitutionalization, Doctrine of Proportionality, Due Process Model, Extralegal Factors, Informal Diversion, Juvenile Court Act of 1899, Juvenile Delinquency, Juvenile Delinquency Prevention Act of 1968, Parens Patriae, Parole Board, Partisan Politics, Policy, Politicized, Politics, Preponderance of the Evidence, Sheriff, Static, Waiver

Section 2.3: The Policymaking role of the Supreme Court

Learning Objectives

After completing this section, you should be able to:

2.3(a) Explain the concept of judicial review.
2.3(b) Describe the composition of the Supreme Court.
2.3(c) Identify the differences between the Warren, Burger, and Rehnquist courts.
2.3(d) Define judicial activism and outline the arguments for and against it.
2.3(e) Explain how the terms liberal and conservative are applied to the high courts and the decisions of those courts.

Introduction

The Supreme Court of the United States has an extremely important policymaking role, and this has an enormous impact on the criminal justice system. As discussed in a previous section, the Supreme Court has the power of judicial review. This power was first exercised in the landmark case of *Marbury v. Madison*, decided in 1803. In that case, the Court struck down a statute that it considered "repugnant to the Constitution." This case served as the precedent for judicial review, and the Supreme Court has exercised the power ever since that time. Judicial review, then, is the authority of the Supreme Court to review the acts of Congress, and determine if those acts meet the standards set forth in the Constitution. It is interesting that the power of judicial review was never directly vested in the court in the text of the Constitution. The Court (in the *Marbury v. Madison* decision) inferred the power for itself.

Recall that the Supreme Court has the judicial power to interpret the law. This provides yet another method for the Supreme Court to make criminal justice policy. The Due Process Clause has proven very important in the Court's shaping of policy through this power. What exactly constitutes due process is extremely vague, and when the Court decides whether something is required by due process, they are in effect making policy. The evolution of police procedure during the Warren Court years is an enduring example of this policy-making power at work.

In theory, Supreme Court justices should practice what constitutional scholars have called judicial modesty. Judicial modesty refers to the idea that justices should only strike down acts of the legislative branch when those laws are in direct conflict with a constitutional provision. There has been a historical trend of judicial self-restraint among at least some justices. These justices feel that policy is best left in the hands of the legislative and executive branches. Striking down a law merely because a majority of justices disagrees with the legislature is wrong under this doctrine. The way our system functions, there is nothing to stop the justices from doing this. Other justices take the position that the court should be active in cases of civil liberties and civil rights. When it comes to allowing political agendas enter into the judicial decision-making process, the justices must police themselves.

Political Tendencies

Supreme Court justices, in theory, sit in order to interpret the law. This interpretation is, in reality, filtered through a political lens. No matter how well meaning these justices may be, their perceptions of what is right or wrong in the law are impacted by their personal political beliefs. While there are always individual differences, a common way to divide the political leanings of the court is to use the terms **liberal** and **conservative** to describe both individual justices, the court in general, and particular decisions.

Illustrations of **liberal decisions** are decisions favoring criminal defendants, people claiming discrimination, and those claiming violations of civil rights. Decisions that appear to favoring police, prosecutors, and other governmental entities are said to be **conservative**.

Currently, the Supreme Court as a distinct cluster of four judges that consistently vote liberal, and another cluster of four justices that vote conservative. Justice Anthony Kennedy sits right in the middle of the political spectrum, and is the "swing" vote that makes predicting the outcome of Supreme Court decisions very difficult.

Not all liberal justices are equally liberal. In the 2013 term, Justices Ruth Bader Ginsburg, Sonia Sotomayor, and Elena Kagan cast liberal votes 70 percent of the time. While still left leaning, Justice Stephen Breyer is substantially more conservative than his female counterparts.

Judicial Activism versus Judicial Restraint

There are two major vantage points from which to regard the work of the Supreme Court. The first is that the constitution should be interpreted as it is written. A second is that the Constitution must be interpreted in the context of modern life and modern problems. The is debate has been characterized as one between **judicial activism** and **judicial restraint**. Judicial activism represents the idea that the Court should actively seek to right wrongs that other branches of government actively promote or will not do anything about. The majority of justices on the Warren Court were known as judicial activists. These justices believed that the court should take an active role in ensuring the civil rights of all Americans. Judicial restraint, on the other hand, is the idea that the democratic process should direct changes in policy. That is, policy should be set by legislative enactments that represent the will of the people. Advocates of judicial restraint commonly argue that since Justices are appointed rather than elected, they are not the proper body to make policy changes. Note that while the Warren court was liberal in its judicial activism, that court's example should not lead to the conclusion that activism is always liberal. The reality is that there will always be a tug of war between a strict constructionist view of the constitution and the dynamic body of ideas envisioned by extreme judicial activists. The reality of an evolving society utilizing evolving technology dictates that the Constitution be somewhat dynamic. The modern history of the Fourth Amendment demonstrates this. A literal interpretation of the constitution would indicate that your phone calls, texts, and emails are all subject to "seizure" by the government without a warrant. Those things did not exist when the Fourth Amendment was written, so they could not be protected. The fundamental question that remains is one of striking a balance between nullifying the democratic process and not allowing the Constitution to remain relevant over time.

The legal framework that judges work within limits judicial activism to some extent. Before a federal court can hear a case, certain conditions must be met. Under the Constitution, federal courts exercise only judicial powers. This means that federal judges may interpret the law only through the resolution of actual legal disputes, referred to in Article III of the Constitution as "Cases or Controversies." A court cannot attempt to correct a problem on its own initiative (unless it has to do with the rules governing the court systems), or to answer a hypothetical legal question. Second, assuming there is an actual case or controversy, the plaintiff in a federal lawsuit also must have legal **standing** to ask the court for a decision. That means the plaintiff must have been aggrieved, or legally harmed in some way, by the defendant. Thus, organizations such as the American Civil Liberties Union cannot sue the police directly, but they can fund legal assistance for a party that actually alleges harm done by the police. In addition, the case must present a category of dispute that the law in question was designed to address, and it must be a complaint that the court has the power to remedy. That is, the court must be authorized, under the Constitution or a federal law, to hear the case. For example, if there is no substantial federal question, the Supreme Court cannot review a case originating in state courts. In addition, the case cannot be **moot**. A case is moot if it does not present an ongoing problem for the court to resolve. The federal courts, thus, are courts of **limited jurisdiction** because they may only decide certain types of cases as provided by Congress or as identified in the Constitution.

Even with these limits, the policymaking role of the Supreme Court should not be underestimated. The rulings of the court are just as consequential as acts of congress and the executive decisions of the president. Many times, the ruling of the court is not based merely on a literal reading of the law. In many cases, the justices are invoking their own interpretations of what the law should be, and not what it objectively is.

Key Terms

American Civil Liberties Union, Article III, Conservative, Conservative Decisions, Judicial Activism, Judicial Restraint, Justice Anthony Kennedy, Justice Elena Kagan, Justice Ruth Bader Ginsburg, Justice Sonia Sotomayor, Justice Stephen Breyer, Liberal, Liberal Decisions, Limited Jurisdiction, Marbury v. Madison (1803), Moot, Right to Counsel, Standing, Warren Court

Section 2.4: The Civil Rights Revolution

Learning Objectives

After completing this section, you should be able to:

2.4(a) Explain the meaning of due process of law, and identify where due process guarantees can be found in American law.

2.4(b) Define the Civil Rights Revolution and provide examples of case law that altered criminal justice procedure.

2.4(c) Describe the effects of *Furman v. Georgia* and *Gregg v. Georgia* on the use of the death penalty in American criminal justice.

2.4(d) Describe the impact of the Rehnquist Court's decisions on the civil rights cases of the Warren Court.

2.4(e) Explain how the Warren Court's decisions fundamentally altered juvenile justice process in the United States providing example cases.

Introduction

A political pendulum, swinging back and forth from liberal to conservative, marks the history of the U.S. Supreme Court. Obviously, conservative courts are courts composed of conservative justices, usually appointed by conservative presidents. Liberal courts, on the other hand, are composed of liberal justices, usually appointed by liberal presidents. These courts are often characterized by the name of the chief justice at the time. During the 1960s, the pendulum swung to the apex of liberalism when Chief Justice Earl Warren (1953 – 1969) led it. The Warren Court adhered to Packer's *Due Process Model*, at least after the judicial activists achieved a majority on the Court with the retirement of Justice Frankfurter's retirement in 1962. This date marks the true beginning of the **civil rights revolution**. This liberal court, headed by Warren, emphasized civil rights across the legal spectrum. The most enduring changes in criminal justice occurred in their interpretations of the **Fourth Amendment** and Fifth Amendments, with many landmark cases coming down that were designed by the court to shield citizens from the abuse of police powers.

Prior to the 1960's, the Supreme Court rarely interfered in the way that states ran their own criminal justice systems. The 1960s was a time of rapid social change, and that change is reflected in the decisions of the Warren Court. When the Warren court passed down its decision in **Mapp v. Ohio** in 1961, the criminal justice system in America was changed forever. However, this was only the beginning. Over the remainder of Warren's tenure as Chief Justice, the court would hand down many more decisions that would redefine the American legal landscape in terms of civil liberties.

A more conservative Supreme Court, back in 1949, stated that the exclusionary rule applied only to federal law enforcement officers. According to the ruling in **Wolf v. Colorado (1949)**, if citizens had any protection against illegally obtained evidence being used against them in court, it was up to state supreme courts to interpret state constitutions in such a way. Many courts did implement the exclusionary rule on the state level, following the lead of the U.S. Supreme Court, but some did not. When *Mapp* overruled *Wolf*, the exclusionary rule was applied to all law enforcement in the United States, no matter what level of government employed them.

Another landmark decision influencing law enforcement practice passed down by the Supreme Court was **Chimel v. California (1969)**. Today, we teach that *Chimel* established an exception to the warrant requirement known as a search incident to arrest. As an exception to the search warrant requirement, this may seem like a case that fits Packer's *crime control model*. This is because an exception to the search warrant requirement is generally considered to benefit law enforcement, and is thus a victory for law and order at the expense of a civil right. The facts of the case paint a different picture. When the police arrested Chimel in his home for burglary, they searched his home for stolen coins that were the fruits of his crime. The coins were found in a garage attached to the house. The court ruled that while the search was incident to the arrest, the search of the garage went too far. The proper scope of a search incident to arrest was the area in the suspect's "immediate control." We can see from this that the court limited a common police practice, effectively doing away with an unwritten arrest exception to the search warrant requirement of the Fourth Amendment. Because this was deemed a due process issue by the Supreme Court, that clause of the Fourteenth Amendment was used to apply the Fourth Amendment rule to state law enforcement.

While the decisions of the Warren court had a weighty impact on many aspects of American life, the most profound effects on the criminal justice system were in the area of due process and defendants' rights. In *Gideon v. Wainwright* (1963), the court held that indigent defendants facing jail time had the right to appointed counsel if they could not afford their own lawyer. In *Miranda v. Arizona* (1966), the Warren Court ruled that police must inform suspects of certain rights prior to a custodial interrogation. Due to popular culture, most every American knows the statement that is read to suspects by the police: *"You have the right to remain silent. Anything you say can and will be used against you in a court of law. You have the right to have an attorney present during questioning. If you cannot afford an attorney, one will be appointed for you by the state."*

Not every case decided by the Warren Court served to benefit criminal defendants. In *Terry v. Ohio* (1968), for example, the Court ruled that the police could search suspects for weapons with less than probable cause.

The pendulum began to swing the other way in the 1970s. This swing occurred because the composition of the court began to change. As liberal justices retired from the court, Republican presidents such as Nixon, Reagan, and Bush replaced them. By the end of the first Bush administration, the court had transitioned from the very liberal Warren Court to a much more conservative body. These conservative courts hammered out many exceptions to the blanket protections created by the Warren Court. This has created an increasingly broad scope of lawful investigative activity for law enforcement. This shift from the Due Process Model to the Crime Control Model did not take place only within the courts. It took place in the executive and the legislative branches as well.

The **Burger Court** (1969 – 1986) was far more conservative than the Warren Court, but there was no conservative majority. One of the most controversial cases decided by the Burger Court was *Furman v. Georgia* (1972), which abolished the death penalty as it was enacted at the time. This was not in keeping with the conservative expectations of the Burger Court because Warren Burger was a conservative appointed by President Richard Nixon. Conservatives hoped that a court led by Burger would be far more conservative, even to the point of overruling the more liberal of the Warren Court's rulings. This was not to happen. The court may have chipped away at the major Warren Court doctrines, but it declined to overturn them. The chief justice may have been conservative when *Furman* was handed down, but the remnants of the Warren Court still sitting on the bench kept the court liberal, at least to a degree, in its majority decisions. Because the composition of the court had shifted, some conservative decisions were handed down. Burger voted with the majority of the court in 1976 to reinstate the death penalty in *Gregg v. Georgia* (1976).

The **Rehnquist Court** (1986 - 2005) was far more conservative than the Burger Court. These conservative courts, perhaps out of concern for the time-honored tradition of cohesion and unity of the Supreme Court, did not overrule many of the liberal decisions of the Warren Court. Rather, they "chipped away" at them by creating scores of exclusions. That is, things like the exclusionary rule still existed as a matter of law, but there would be many exceptions that were created during the Reagan-Bush years.

Conservatives applauded this as strengthening the ability of the police to do their jobs, and liberals lamented it as the erosion of hard-won civil liberties.

Rehnquist was a strong believer in states' rights. Much of his decisionmaking hinged on the Tenth Amendment's reservation of powers to state government. He also rejected the broad view of the Fourteenth Amendment taken by the Warren Court and believed that such an interpretation overstepped the proper bounds of federal power. An example of the chipping away at liberal interpretations of the fourth amendment is *Maryland v. Garrison* (1987). In this case, the court held that a search pursuant to a warrant that the police believed incorrectly to be valid did not violate the searched person's Fourth Amendment Rights. This **good faith exception** meant that such evidence could be admitted at trial. Another example is *California v. Greenwood* (1988), in which the court ruled that a warrant was not necessary to search a garbage can left on the curb for pickup (outside the curtilage of the home).

Juveniles and Civil Rights

Before the 1960s, few people challenged the sweeping powers of the juvenile justice system. During the Civil Rights Revolution, the Supreme Court considered the rights of juveniles at the time and found them wanting. In a series of fundamental cases, the Supreme Court greatly expanded the rights of juveniles. Many critics point out that these changes made the juvenile justice system look a lot more like the adult system.

In the landmark case of *In Re Gault* (1967), the Supreme Court extended many due process rights enjoyed by adults accused of a crime to juveniles. The facts of the case were rather shocking: A 15-year old boy named Gerald Gault had been sentenced to six years in a state "training school" for making a prank phone call. If Gerald had been an adult, the maximum penalty for this offense would have been a maximum fine of $50 and a maximum jail sentence of two months. As most juvenile cases proceeded at that time, Gerald was convicted and sentenced in a shockingly (by today's standards) informal proceeding without the benefit of a lawyer. In reviewing the case, the court determined that all juveniles risking incarceration had the fundamental rights to have a lawyer for their defense, to confront and examine their accusers in court, and to have adequate notice of the charges against them.

In re Gault represented the beginning of a long series of cases where the court extended rights enjoyed by adults in the criminal justice system to children in the juvenile justice system. In *In Re Winship* (1970), the court established that the state must establish guilt "beyond a reasonable doubt" as it was in adult courts. In *Breed v. Jones* (1975) the Court extended the constitutional protection against Double Jeopardy to juveniles when it ruled that juveniles cannot be found delinquent in juvenile court and then transferred to adult court without a hearing on the transfer. There were limits to the number of adult rights that the court was willing to extend to juveniles. In *McKeiver v. Pennsylvania* (1971), the Supreme Court determined that juveniles do not have the right to a trial by jury.

During the "get tough on crime" era of the 1980s, juveniles were not immune to toughening sanctions. Legislators made similar changes to the juvenile justice system as they had to the adult system. In *Schall v. Martin* (1984) for example, the court determined that juveniles could be held in preventive detention if it was determined that they posed a risk of committing additional crimes while awaiting action by the courts. There was also a broadening of the range of juveniles that qualified for waiver to adult criminal court.

Key Terms

Breed v. Jones (1975), Burger Court (1969 -1986), *California v. Greenwood* (1988), *Chimel v. California* (1969), Civil Rights Revolution, Fourth Amendment, *Furman v. Georgia* (1972), *Gideon v. Wainwright* (1963), Good Faith Exception, *Gregg v. Georgia* (1976), *In Re Gault* (1967), *In Re Winship* (1970), *Mapp v. Ohio* (1961), *Maryland v. Garrison* (1987), *McKeiver v. Pennsylvania* (1971), *Miranda v. Arizona* (1966), *Rehnquist Court* (1986-2005), *Schall v. Martin* (1984), Search Incident to Arrest, *Terry v. Ohio* (1968), *Wolf v. Colorado* (1949)

Section 2.5: Theories of Punishment

Learning Objectives

After completing this section, you should be able to:

2.5(a)   Explain the concept of deterrence, and explain the elements necessary for it to work under rational choice theory.

2.5(b)   Describe the concept of incapacitation and problems associated with it in criminal justice practice.

2.5(c)   Explain rehabilitation as a goal of punishment, and provide examples of rehabilitation programs.

2.5(d)   Explain the idea of retribution in criminal justice philosophy, and how it relates to the idea of just deserts.

2.5(e)   Describe evidence offered to demonstrate that both individual racism and institutional racism exist within criminal justice in America.

Introduction

When it comes to criminal sanctions, what people believe to be appropriate is largely determined by the theory of punishment to which they subscribe. That is, people tend to agree with the theory of punishment that is most likely to generate the outcome they believe is the correct one. This system of beliefs about the purposes of punishment often spills over into the political arena. Politics and correctional policy are intricately related. Many of the changes seen in corrections policy in the United States during this time were a reflection of the political climate of the day. During the more liberal times of the 1960s and 1970s, criminal sentences were largely the domain of the judicial and executive branches of government. The role of the legislatures during this period was to design sentencing laws with rehabilitation as the primary goal. During the politically conservative era of the 1980s and 1990s, lawmakers took much of that power away from the judicial and executive branches. Much of the political rhetoric of this time was about "getting tough on crime." The correctional goals of retribution, incapacitation, and deterrence became dominate, and rehabilitation was shifted to a distant position.

Deterrence

It has been a popular notion throughout the ages that fear of punishment can reduce or eliminate undesirable behavior. This notion has always been popular among criminal justice thinkers. These ideas have been formalized in several different ways. The Utilitarian philosopher Jeremy Bentham is credited with articulating the three elements that must be present if deterrence is to work: The punishment must be administered with celerity, certainty, and appropriate severity. These elements are applied under a type **rational choice theory**. Rational choice theory is the simple idea that people think about committing a crime before they do it. If the rewards of the crime outweigh the punishment, then they do the prohibited act. If the punishment is seen as outweighing the rewards, then they do not do it. Sometimes criminologists borrow the phrase **cost-benefit analysis** from economists to describe this sort of decision-making process.

When evaluating whether deterrence works or not, it is important to differentiate between general deterrence and specific deterrence. General deterrence is the idea that every person punished by the law serves as an example to others contemplating the same unlawful act. Specific deterrence is the idea that the individuals punished by the law will not commit their crimes again because they "learned a lesson."

Critics of deterrence theory point to high **recidivism** rates as proof that the theory does not work. Recidivism means a relapse into crime. In other words, those who are punished by the criminal justice system tend to reoffend at a very high rate. Some critics also argue that rational choice theory does not work. They argue that such things as crimes of passion and crimes committed by those under the influence of drugs and alcohol are not the product of a rational cost-benefit analysis.

As unpopular as rational choice theories may be with particular schools of modern academic criminology, they are critically important to understanding how the criminal justice system works. This is because nearly *the entire criminal justice system is based on rational choice theory*. The idea that people commit crimes because they decide to do so is the very foundation of criminal law in the United States. In fact, the intent element must be proven beyond a reasonable doubt in almost every felony known to American criminal law before a conviction can be secured. Without a **culpable mental state**, there is no crime (with very few exceptions).

Incapacitation

Incapacitation is a very pragmatic goal of criminal justice. The idea is that if criminals are locked up in a secure environment, they cannot go around victimizing everyday citizens. The weakness of incapacitation is that it works only as long as the offender is locked up. There is no real question that incapacitation reduces crime by some degree. The biggest problems with incapacitation is the cost. There are high social and moral costs when the criminal justice system takes people out of their homes, away from their families, and out of the workforce and lock them up for a protracted period. In addition, there are massive financial costs with this model. Very long prison sentences result in very large prison populations that require a very large prison industrial complex. These expenses have placed a crippling financial burden on many states.

Rehabilitation

Rehabilitation is a noble goal of punishment by the state that seeks to help the offender become a productive, noncriminal member of society. Throughout history, there have been several different notions as to how this help should be administered. When our modern correctional system was forming, this was the dominant model. We can see by the very name *corrections* that the idea was to help the offender become a non-offender. Education programs, faith-based programs, drug treatment programs, anger management programs, and many others are aimed at helping the offender "get better."

Overall, rehabilitation efforts have had poor results when measured by looking at recidivism rates. Those that the criminal justice system tried to help tend to reoffend at about the same rate as those who serve prison time without any kind of treatment. Advocates of rehabilitation point out that past efforts failed because they were underfunded, ill-conceived, or poorly executed. Today's drug courts are an example of how we may be moving back toward a more rehabilitative model, especially with first-time and nonviolent offenders.

Retribution

Retribution means giving offenders the punishment they deserve. Most adherents to this idea believe that the punishment should fit the offense. This idea is known as the **doctrine of proportionality**. Such a doctrine was advocated by early Italian criminologist **Cesare Beccaria,** who viewed the harsh punishments of his day as being disproportionate to many of the crimes committed. The term **just desert** is often used to describe a deserved punishment that is proportionate to the crime committed.

In reality, the doctrine of proportionality is difficult to achieve. There is no way that the various legislatures can go about objectively measuring criminal culpability. The process is one of legislative consensus and is imprecise at best.

A Racist System?

The United States today can be described as both multiracial and multiethnic. This has led to **racism**. Racism is the belief that members of one race are inferior to members of another race. Because white Americans of European heritage are the majority, racism in America usually takes on the character of whites against racial and ethnic minorities. Historically, these ethnic minorities have not been given equal footing on such important aspects of life as employment, housing, education, healthcare, and criminal justice. When this unequal treatment is willful, it can be referred to as **racial discrimination**. The law forbids racial discrimination in the criminal justice system, just as it does in the workplace.

Disproportionate minority contact refers to the disproportionate number of minorities who come into contact with the criminal justice system. Disproportionate minority contact is a problem in both the adult and juvenile systems at every level of those systems. As the gatekeepers of the criminal justice system, the police are often accused of discriminatory practices.

Courts are not immune to cries of racism from individuals and politically active groups. The American Civil Liberties Union (2014), for example, states, "African-Americans are incarcerated for drug offenses at a rate that is 10 times greater than that of whites."

The literature on disproportionate minority sentencing distinguishes between legal and **extralegal factors**. Legal factors are those things that we accept as legitimately, as a matter of law, mitigating or aggravating criminal sentences. Such things as the seriousness of the offense and the defendant's prior criminal record fall into this category. Extralegal factors include things like class, race, and gender. These are regarded as illegitimate factors in determining criminal sentences. They have nothing to do with the defendant's criminal behavior, and everything to do with the defendant's status as a member of a particular group.

One way to measure racial disparity is to compare the proportion of people that are members of a particular group (their proportion in the general population) with the proportion or that group at a particular stage in the criminal justice system. In 2013, the Bureau of the Census (Bureau of the Census, 2014) estimated that African-Americans made up 13.2% of the population of the United States. According to the FBI, 28.4% of all arrestees were African-American. From this information, we can see that the proportion of African-Americans arrested was just over double what one would expect.

The disparity is more pronounced when it comes to drug crime. According to the NAACP (2014), "African Americans represent 12% of the total population of drug users, but 38% of those arrested for drug offenses, and 59% of those in state prison for a drug offense."

There are three basic explanations for these disparities in the criminal justice system. The first is **individual racism**. Individual racism refers to a particular person's beliefs, assumptions, and behaviors. This type of racism manifests itself when the individual police officer, defense attorney, prosecutor, judge, parole board member, or parole officer is bigoted. Another explanation of racial disparities in the criminal justice system is **institutional racism**. Institutional racism manifests itself when departmental policies (both formal and informal), regulations, and laws result in unfair treatment of a particular group. A third (and controversial) explanation is differential involvement in crime. The basic idea is that African-Americans and Hispanics are involved in more criminal activity. Often this is tied to social problems such as poor education, poverty, and unemployment.

While it does not seem that bigotry is present in every facet of the criminal and juvenile justice systems, it does appear that there are pockets of prejudice within both systems. It is difficult to deny the data: Discrimination does take place in such areas as use of force by police and the imposition of the death penalty. Historically, nowhere was the disparity more discussed and debated than in federal drug policy. While much has recently changed with the passage of the **Fair Sentencing Act of 2010**, federal drug law was a prime example of institutional racism at work.

Under former law, crimes involving crack cocaine were punished much, much more severely than powder cocaine. The law had certain harsh penalties that were triggered by weight, and a provision that required one hundred times more powder than crack. Many deemed the law racist because the majority of arrests for crack cocaine were of African-Americans, and the majority of arrests for powder cocaine were white. African-American defendants have appealed their sentences based on Fourteenth Amendment equal protection claims.

Key Terms

Celerity, Certainty, Cesare Beccaria, Cost Benefit Analysis, Culpable Mental State, Deterrence, Disproportionate Minority Contact, Drug Court, Fair Sentencing Act of 2010, General Deterrence, Incapacitation, Individual Racism, Institutional Racism, Multiethnic Multiracial, NAACP, Racial Discrimination, Racism, Rational Choice Theory, Recidivism Rehabilitation, Retribution, Severity, Specific Deterrence

Chapter 3: Criminal Law

The term *criminal law* can be confusing. This is because some sources use it in a very general way to describe the entire spectrum of laws dealing with the criminal justice system; others use it as a shorthand way of referring to what is also known as the **substantive criminal law**. This text follows the latter approach by using the heading criminal law to refer to the substantive criminal law, which is the part of the law that describes what acts are prohibited and what punishments are associated with those acts. Also included are legal defenses (such as the insanity defense) that apply in criminal cases.

A common way of organizing criminal laws is to divide them into *felonies* and *misdemeanors*, which depend largely on the seriousness of the offense and the type of punishment associated with the offense. Things like petty thefts, simple assault, disorderly conduct, and public drunkenness are relatively nonserious crimes classified as **misdemeanors**. Misdemeanors are usually only punishable by fine and imprisonment in a local jail for a period less than a year. **Felonies**, on the other hand, are serious crimes (e.g., rape, murder, burglary, kidnapping) where the punishment can be death or a long period (at least a year) of incarceration in a state-run prison. Note that this distinction depends on the sentence; some convicts go to prison for less than a year because of early release programs such as "good time" and parole.

There is also a distinction between types of criminal law based in the inherent evil of the act. If the act is "wrong in itself," it is considered a *mala in se* offense. If an act is not necessarily evil and is only considered criminal because it is prohibited by the government, it is considered a *mala prohibita* offense. Most so-called "victimless crimes" are *mala prohibita* offenses. Because people's views vary so widely as to the inherent wrongness of an act, there is no absolute standard for classification.

Criminal acts that are highly visible to the public are often referred to as **visible crime, ordinary crime,** or **street crime.** The overt nature of such crimes makes notice by police more likely, and thus prosecution more likely. Murder is a common example: Most murders come to the attention of the police, and prosecution is more likely than for most other offenses. Occupational crimes are less obvious. These are crimes that a particular job provides the criminal opportunity. The most common example is **embezzlement.** Crimes committed by groups with a discernable organization structure are classified as **organized crime.** Organized crime is considered especially heinous because groups can cause more criminal damage, and the groups make for more difficult investigations and prosecutions.

A large swath of criminal offenses involving computers and related technologies are collectively known as **cybercrime.** Cybercrime involves disparate acts such as distributing child pornography, sending out mass emails in an attempt to obtain identifying information (**phishing**), distributing viruses designed to damage computer systems, hacking into business computers to steal money, and so forth.

Crimes that are motivated by bias toward a particular race, religion, ethnicity, or sexuality are known as **hate crimes**.

Criminal versus Civil Law

At civil law, a wrong done to another person is called a **tort**. When a harmed individual (the plaintiff) wins a tort case in civil court, they may also win a money award referred to as **damages**. In other words, torts are private wrongs. A criminal prosecution operates under a different legal theory. A crime, the theory holds, may harm the individual, but it also harms all of society. Since the people are represented by the state, all criminal prosecutions are brought forward in the name of the state. What the "state" calls itself can vary from state to state; some prosecutions are done in the name of the people, and some are done in the name of the "commonwealth." Regardless of how the case is named, a prosecutor working for the government on behalf of society brings it forward.

It is important to note that the criminal system and the civil system sometimes interact. A person can be found guilty of a crime in criminal court, and found liable for a tort for the exact same behavior. In addition, individuals that have suffered losses due to criminal actions can sometimes use the civil courts to recoup their losses.

State versus Federal Crimes

While the United States is a common law country, most criminal laws are a matter of statutes today. An essential difference between a state criminal statute and a federal criminal statute is that federal laws will usually contain a jurisdictional element. Because of the constitutional limits placed on the authority of Congress to make criminal laws, federal criminal statutes must be tailored to a particular power delegated to Congress, such as the power to regulate interstate commerce. Most criminal laws exist on the state level because of this limitation.

When a particular act is criminal on both the state and federal level, there is overlapping jurisdiction in the case. As a matter of constitutional law, the person could be prosecuted on both the state and federal level. In practice, this rarely happens. In a few high-profile cases, federal prosecutors have taken up a case when the public widely perceived that justice was not done in state courts (e.g., the Rodney King police brutality case).

Section 3.1: Sources of Criminal Law

Learning Objectives

After completing this section, you should be able to:

3.1(a)   Describe the development of the common law and how it came to the United States.
3.1(b)   Describe the doctrine of stare decisis and its impact on the American legal system.
3.1(c)   Identify the various sources of law in America, and describe the nature of each.
3.1(d)   List and describe the limits placed on criminal statutes by the Constitution of the United States.
3.1(e)   Describe the origins and content of the Model Penal Code.
3.1(f)   Compare and contrast the civil law with the criminal law.

Introduction

The primary function of the substantive criminal law is to define crimes, including the associated punishment. The **procedural criminal law** sets the procedures for arrests, searches and seizures, and interrogations. In addition, it establishes the rules for conducting trials. Where does criminal law come from?

The Common Law

The term *common law* can be disturbingly vague for the student. That is because different sources use it in several different ways with subtle differences in meaning. The best way to get a grasp on the term's meaning is to understand a little of the history of the American legal system. Common law, which some sources refer to as "judge-made" law, first appeared when judges decided cases based on the legal customs of medieval England at the time. It may be hard for us to imagine today, but in the early days of English common law, the law was a matter of *oral* tradition. That is, the definitions of crimes and associated punishments were not written down in a way that gave them binding authority.

By the end of the medieval period, some of these cases were recorded in written form. Over a period, imported judicial decisions became recorded on a regular basis and collected into books called **reporters**. The English-speaking world is forever indebted to Sir William Blackstone, an English legal scholar, for collecting much of the common law tradition of England and committing it to paper in an organized way. His four-volume set, **Commentaries on the Laws of England**, was taken to the colonies by the founding fathers. The founding fathers incorporated the common law of England into the laws of the Colonies, and ultimately into the laws of the United States.

In modern America, most crimes are defined by statute. These statutory definitions use ideas and terms that come from the common law tradition. When judges take on the task of interpreting a statute, they still use common law principles for guidance. The definitions of many crimes, such as murder and arson, have not deviated much from their common law origin. Other crimes, such as rape, have seen sweeping changes.

One of the primary characteristics of the common law tradition is the importance of **precedent**. Known by the legal Latin phrase **stare decisis**, the doctrine of precedence means that once a court makes a decision on a particular matter, they are bound to rule the same way in future cases that have the same legal issue. This is important because a consistent ruling in identical factual situations means that everyone gets the same treatment by the courts. In other words, the doctrine of *stare decisis* ensures equal treatment under the law.

Constitutions

When the founding fathers signed the Constitution, they all agreed that it would be the supreme law of the land; the Framers stated this profoundly important agreement in Article VI. After the landmark case of *Marbury v. Madison* (1803), the Supreme Court has had the power to strike down any law or any government action that violates constitutional principles. This precedent means that any law made by the Congress of the United States or the legislative assembly of any state that does not meet constitutional standards is subject to nullification by the Supreme Court of the United States.

Every state adopted this idea of constitutional supremacy when creating their constitutions. All state laws are subject to review by the high courts of those states. If a state law or government practice (e.g., police, courts, or corrections) violates the constitutional law of that state, then it will be struck down by that state's high court. Local laws are subject to similar scrutiny.

Statutory Law

Statutes are written laws passed by legislative assemblies. Modern criminal laws tend to be a matter of statutory law. In other words, most states and the federal government have moved away from the common-law definitions of crimes and established their own versions through the legislative process. Thus, most of the criminal law today is made by state legislatures, with the federal criminal law being made by Congress. Legislative assemblies tend to consider legislation as it is presented, not in subject order. This chronological ordering makes finding the law concerning a particular matter very difficult. To simplify finding the law, most all statutes are organized by subject in a set of books called a code. The body of statutes that comprises the criminal law is often referred to as the criminal code, or less commonly as the penal code.

Administrative Law

The clear distinction between the executive, legislative, and judicial branches of government becomes blurry when U.S. governmental agencies and commissions are considered. These types of bureaucratic organizations can be referred to as semi-legislative and semi-judicial in character. These organizations have the power to make rules that have the force of law, the power to investigation violations of those laws, and the power to impose sanctions on those deemed to be in violation. Examples of such agencies are the Federal Trade Commission (FTC), the Internal Revenue Service (IRS), and the Environmental Protection Agency (EPA). When these agencies make rules that have the force of law, the rules are collectively referred to as **administrative law**.

Court Cases

When the appellate courts decide a legal issue, the doctrine of precedence means that future cases must follow that decision. This means that the holding in an appellate court case has the force of law. Such laws are often referred to as **case law**. The entire criminal justice community depends on the appellate courts, especially the Supreme Court, to evaluate and clarify both statutory laws and government practices against the requirements of the Constitution. These legal rules are all set down in court cases.

Key Terms

Administrative Law, Case Law, *Commentaries on the Laws of England*, Criminal Law, Cybercrime, Damages, Embezzlement, Felony, Hate Crime, Misdemeanor, Ordinary Crime, Organized Crime, Phishing, Precedent, Procedural Criminal Law, Reporter, Sir William Blackstone, *Stare Decisis*, Street Crime, Substantive Criminal Law, Tort, Visible Crime

Section 3.2: Substantive Criminal Law

Learning Objectives

After completing this section, you should be able to:

3.2(a) Discuss the idea of the rule of law and explain its importance in the American legal system.
3.2(b) Explain the constitutional prohibitions against Bills of Attainder and Ex Post Facto laws.
3.2(c) Explain the limits that the First Amendment places on the criminal law, citing doctrinal examples.
3.2(d) Explain the limits that the Second Amendment places on the criminal law, citing doctrinal examples.
3.2(e) Describe the limits that the Eighth Amendment places on the criminal law, citing doctrinal examples.
3.2(f) Describe the development of the right to privacy in constitutional law.

Introduction

As previously discussed, the criminal law in its broadest sense encompasses both the substantive criminal law and **criminal procedure**. In a more limited sense, the term *criminal law* is used to denote the *substantive criminal law*, and *criminal procedure* is considered another category of law. (Most college criminal justice programs organize classes this way). Recall that the *substantive law* defines criminal acts that the legislature wishes to prohibit and specifies penalties for those that commit the prohibited acts. For example, murder is a substantive law because it prohibits the killing of another human being without justification.

No Crime without Law

It is fundamental to the American way of life that there can be no crime without law. This concept defines the idea of the Rule of Law. The rule of law is the principle that the law should govern a nation, not an individual. The importance of the rule of law in America stems from the colonial experience with the English monarchy. It follows that, in America, no one is above the law.

Constitutional Limits

Unlike the governments of other countries, the legislative assemblies of the United States do not have unlimited power. The power of Congress to enact criminal laws is circumscribed by the Constitution. These limits apply to state legislatures as well.

Bills of Attainder and *Ex Post Facto* Laws. A **bill of attainder** is an enactment by a legislature that declares a person (or a group of people) guilty of a crime and subject to punishment for committing that crime without the benefit of a trial. An ***ex post facto*** law is a law that makes an act done before the legislature enacted the law criminal and punishes that act. The prohibition also forbids the legislature from making the penalty for a crime more severe retroactively. Both of these types of laws are strictly prohibited by the Constitution.

Fair Notice and Vagueness. The due process clauses of the Fifth and Fourteenth Amendments mandate that the criminal law afford **fair notice**. The idea of fair notice is that people must be able to determine exactly what is prohibited by the law, so vague and ambiguous laws are prohibited. If a law is determined to be unclear by the Supreme Court, it will be struck down and declared **void for vagueness**. Such laws would allow for arbitrary and discriminatory enforcement if allowed to stand.

First Amendment

The First Amendment to the United States Constitution guarantees all Americans the "freedom of expression." Among these "expressions" are the freedom of religion and the freedom of speech. In general, Americans can say pretty much whatever they like without fear of punishment. Any criminal law passed by the legislature that infringes on these rights would not withstand constitutional scrutiny. There are, however, some exceptions.

When the health and safety of the public are at issue, the government can curtail the freedom of speech. One of the most commonly cited limiting principles is what has been called the **clear and present danger test**. This test, established by the Supreme Court in *Schenck v. United States* (1919), prohibits inherently dangerous speech, such as falsely shouting "fire!" in a crowded theater.

Another prohibited type of speech has been referred to as **fighting words**. This means that the First Amendment does not protect speech calculated to incite a violent reaction. Other types of unprotected speech include hate speech, profanity, libelous utterances, and obscenity. These latter types of speech are very difficult to regulate by law because they are very hard to define and place limits on. The current trend has been to protect more speech that would have once been considered obscene or profane.

The freedom to worship as one sees fit is also enshrined in the Constitution. Appellate courts will strike down statutes that are designed to restrict this **freedom of religion**. The high court has protected door-to-door solicitations by religious groups and even ritualistic animal sacrifices. The Court, however, has not upheld all claims based on the free exercise of religion. Statutes criminalizing such things as snake handling, polygamy, and the use of hallucinogenic drugs have all been upheld.

The First Amendment protects the right of the people to assemble publicly, but as with the other freedoms previously discussed, it is not absolute. The courts have upheld restrictions on the time, place, and manner of public assemblies, so long as those restrictions were deemed reasonable. The reasonableness of such restrictions usually hinges on a **compelling state interest**. The **freedom of assembly**, then, does not protect conduct that jeopardizes the public health and safety.

Second Amendment

The constitutionally guaranteed "right to keep and bear arms" in the Second Amendment is by no means absolute has been the source of much litigation and political debate in recent years. The Supreme Court has established that the second Amendment confers a right to the carrying of a firearm for self-defense, and that right is applicable via the Fourteenth Amendment to the states. Typical restrictions include background checks and waiting periods. Some jurisdictions highly regulate the concealing, carrying, and purchase of firearms and many limit the type of firearms that can be purchased. Many criminal laws have enhanced penalties when they are committed with firearms. Most gun laws and **concealed carry laws** vary widely from jurisdiction to jurisdiction.

Eighth Amendment

The **Eighth Amendment** to the United States Constitution prohibits the imposition of **Cruel and Unusual Punishments**. Both the terms *cruel* and *unusual* do not mean what they mean in everyday usage; they are both legal terms of art. The Supreme Court has incorporated the doctrine of proportionality into the

Eighth Amendment. Recall that *proportionality* means that the punishment should fit the crime, or, at least, should not be grossly disproportionate to the offense. The idea of proportionality has appeared in cases that considered the grading of offenses, the validity of lengthy prison sentences, and whether the imposition of the death penalty is constitutional. (The legal controversies of three strikes laws and the death penalty will be discussed at greater length in a later section).

The Right to Privacy

Most American's view the **right to privacy** as a fundamental human right. It is shocking, then, to find that the Constitution *never* expressly mentions a right to privacy. The Supreme Court agrees that such a right is fundamental to due process and has established the right as being inferred from several other guaranteed rights. Among these are the right of free association, the prohibition against quartering soldiers in private homes, and the prohibition against unreasonable searches and seizures. The right to privacy has been used to protect many controversial practices that were (at least at the time) socially unacceptable to large groups of people. Early courts decided that laws prohibiting single people from purchasing contraceptives were unconstitutional based on privacy rights arguments. The right to an abortion established in *Roe v. Wade* (1973) hinged primarily on a privacy rights argument. More recently, in *Lawrence v. Texas* (2003), the court ruled that laws prohibiting private homosexual sexual activity were unconstitutional. In the *Lawrence* case, privacy rights were the deciding factor.

Key Terms

Bill of Attainder, Clear and Present Danger Test, Compelling State Interest, Concealed Carry Law, Criminal Procedure, Cruel and Unusual Punishment, Eighth Amendment, *Ex Post Facto* **Law, Fair Notice, Fighting Words, First Amendment, Freedom of Assembly, Freedom of Expression, Freedom of Religion,** *Lawrence v. Texas* **(2003), Right to Privacy,** *Roe v. Wade* **(1973),** *Schenck v. United States* **(1919), Second Amendment, Void for Vagueness**

Section 3.3: Elements of Crimes

Learning Objectives

After completing this section, you should be able to:

3.3(a)   Describe the *actus reus* element of crimes.
3.3(b)   Describe the *mens rea* element of crimes referencing the four culpable mental states recognized in the Model Penal Code.
3.3(c)   Explain what is meant by strict liability, and given examples of strict liability offenses.
3.3(d)   Define the element of concurrence.
3.3(e)   Differentiate between crimes of general intent and crimes of specific intent.
3.3(f)   Describe the element of harm, and how the element of cause relates to it.

Introduction

The legal definitions of all crimes contain certain **elements**. If the government cannot prove the existence of these elements, it cannot obtain a conviction in a court of law. Other elements are not part of all crimes, but are only found in crimes that prohibit a particular *harm*. Often, a difference in one particular element of a crime can distinguish it from another related offense, or a particular degree of the same offense. At common law, for example, manslaughter was distinguished from murder by the mental element of **malice aforethought**.

The Criminal Act

Nobody can read minds, and the First Amendment means that people can say pretty much whatever they want. What you think and say (within limits) is protected. It is what you do—your behaviors—that the criminal law seeks to regulate. Lawyers use the legal Latin phrase ***actus reus*** to describe this element of a crime. It is commonly translated into English as the *guilty act*. The term *act* can be a bit confusing. Most people tend to think of the term *act* as an action verb—it is something that people do. The criminal law often seeks to punish people for things that they did *not* do. When the law commands people to take a particular action and they do not take the commanded action, it is known as an ***omission***. The law commands that people feed and shelter their children. Those who do not are guilty of an offense based on the omission. The law commands that people pay their income taxes; if they do not pay their taxes, the omission can be criminal. Threatening to act or attempting an act can also be the *actus reus* element of an offense.

In addition to acts and omissions, **possession** of something can be a criminal offense. The possession of certain weapons, illicit drugs, burglary tools, and so forth are all guilty acts as far as the criminal law is concerned. **Actual possession** is the legal idea that most closely coincides with the everyday use of the term. Actual possession refers to a person having physical control or custody of an object. In addition to actual possession, there is the idea of **constructive possession**. Constructive possession is the legal idea that the person had knowledge of the object, as well as the ability to exercise control over it.

Criminal Intent

A fundamental principle of law is that to be convicted of a crime, there must be a guilty act (the *actus reus*) and a culpable mental state. Recall that culpability means blameworthiness. In other words, there are literally hundreds of legal terms that describe mental states that are worthy of blame. The most common is *intent*. The **Model Penal Code** boils all of these different terms into four basic culpable mental states: purposely, knowingly, recklessly, and negligently.

Purposely. According to the Model Penal Code, a person acts **purposely** when "it is his conscious object to engage in conduct of that nature…."

Knowingly. A person acts **knowingly** if "he is aware that it is practically certain that his conduct will cause such a result." In other words, the prohibited result was not the actor's purpose, but he knew it would happen.

Recklessly. A person acts **recklessly** if "he consciously disregards a substantial and unjustifiable risk." Further, "The risk must be of such a nature and degree that, considering the nature and purpose of the actor's conduct and the circumstances known to him, its disregard involves a gross deviation from the standard of conduct that a law-abiding person would observe in the actor's situation."

Negligently. A person acts **negligently** when "he should be aware of a substantial and unjustifiable risk that the material element exists or will result from his conduct." The idea is that a reasonably carefully person would have seen the danger, but the actor did not.

At times, the legislature will purposely exclude the *mens rea* element from a criminal offense. This leaves only the guilty act to define the crime. Crimes with no culpable mental state are known as **strict liability** offenses. Most of the time, such crimes are mere violations such as speeding. An officer does not have to give evidence that you were speeding purposely, just that you were speeding. If violations such as this had a mental element, it would put an undue burden on law enforcement and the lower courts. There are a few instances where serious felony crimes are strict liability, such as the statutory rape laws of many states.

Concurrence

For an act to be a crime, the act must be brought on by the criminal intent. In most cases, concurrence is obvious and does not enter into the legal arguments. A classic example is an individual who breaks into a cabin in the woods to escape the deadly cold outside. After entering, the person decides to steal the owner's property. This would not be a burglary (at common law) since burglary requires a breaking and entering with the intent to commit a felony therein. Upon entry, the intent was to escape the cold, not to steal. Thus, there was no **concurrence** between the guilty mind and the guilty act.

Criminal Harm and Causation

In criminal law, **causation** refers to the relationship between a person's behavior and a negative outcome. Some crimes, such as murder, require a prohibited outcome. There is no murder if no one has died (although there may be an *attempt*). In crimes that require such a prohibited harm, the *actus reus* must have caused that **harm**.

Key Terms

Actual Possession, Actus Reus, Causation, Concurrence, Constructive Possession, Elements (of crimes), Harm, Knowingly, Malice Aforethought, Model Penal Code, Negligently, Omission, Possession, Purposely, Recklessly

Section 3.4: Legal Defenses

Learning Objectives

After completing this section, you should be able to:

3.4(a)   Compare and contrast the two major categories of legal defenses.
3.4(b)   Discuss the frequency and probability of success of the insanity defense.
3.4(c)   List and explain the various legal tests for insanity.
3.4(d)   Describe the circumstances under which intoxication may be a legal defense, and when it is not.
3.4(e)   Describe the circumstances under which a successful entrapment defense can be raised.
3.4(f)   Describe the circumstances under which a successful self-defense justification may be raised.
3.4(g)   Describe the circumstances under which a successful necessity defense may be raised.
3.4(h)   Describe when a mistake is and is not a valid legal defense.

Introduction

To successfully obtain a conviction, the prosecutor must show all of the elements of the crime beyond a reasonable doubt in criminal court. This is not the end of it in some cases. It must also be shown (if the issue is raised) that the *actus reus* and the *mens rea* was present, but also that the defendant committed the act without **justification** or **excuse**. Both justifications and excuses are species of **legal defenses**. If a legal defense is successful, it will either mitigate or eliminate guilt.

A *justification* consists of a permissible reason for committing an act that would otherwise be a crime. Under normal circumstances, for example, it would be a crime to shoot a man dead on the street. If, however, the man was a mugger and had the shooter at knifepoint, then the justification of self-defense could be raised. A justification means that an act would normally be wrong, but under the circumstances it was the right thing to do. An excuse is different. When a criminal defendant uses an excuse, the act was not the right thing to do, but society should nevertheless hold the actor less culpable because of some extenuating circumstance.

The Insanity Defense

The term insanity comes from the law; psychology and medicine do not use it. The everyday use of the term can be misleading. If a person acts abnormally, they tend to be considered by many as "crazy" or "insane." At law, merely having a mental disease or mental defect is not adequate to mitigate guilt. It must be remembered that Jeffery Dahmer was determined to be *legally* sane, even though everyone who knows the details of his horrible acts knows that he was seriously mentally ill. To use insanity as a legal excuse, the defendant has to show that he or she lacked the capacity to understand that the act was wrong, or the capacity to understand the nature of the act. Some jurisdictions have a **not guilty by reason of insanity** plea.

The logic of the **insanity defense** goes back to the idea of *mens rea* and culpability. We as a society usually only want to punish those people who knew what they were doing was wrong. Most people believe that it is morally wrong to punish someone for an unavoidable accident. Likewise, society does not punish very young children for acts that would be crimes if an adult did them. The logic is that they do not have the maturity and wisdom to foresee and understand the nature of the consequences of the act. Put in oversimplified terms, if a person is so crazy that they do not understand that what they are doing is wrong, it is morally wrong to punish them for it.

Over the years, different courts in different jurisdictions have devised different tests to determine systematically if a criminal defendant is legally insane. One of the oldest and most enduring tests is the **M'Naghten rule**, handed down by the English court in 1843. The basis of the M'Naghten test is the inability to distinguish right from wrong. The Alabama Supreme Court, in the case of ***Parsons v. State*** (1887), first adopted the **Irresistible Impulse Test**. The basic idea is that some people, under the duress of a mental illness, cannot control their actions despite understanding that the action is wrong.

Today, all of the federal courts and the majority of state courts use the **substantial capacity test** developed within the *Model Penal Code*. According to this test, a person is not culpable for a criminal act "if at the time of the crime as a result of mental disease or defect the defendant lacked the capacity to appreciate the wrongfulness of his or her conduct or to conform the conduct to the requirements of the law." In other words, this test contains the awareness of wrongdoing standard of M'Naghten as well as the involuntary compulsion standard of the irresistible impulse test.

It is a Hollywood myth that many violent criminals escape justice with the insanity defense. In fact, the insanity defense is seldom attempted by criminal defendants and is very seldom successful when it is used. Of those who do successfully use it, most of them spend more time in mental institutions than they would have spent in prison had they been convicted. The insanity defense is certainly no "get out of jail free card."

Entrapment

Entrapment is a defense that removes blame from a person who commits a criminal act when convinced to do so by law enforcement. In other words, people have the defense of entrapment available when police lure them into crime. A valid entrapment defense has two related elements: There must be a government inducement of the crime, and the defendant's lack of predisposition to engage in the criminal conduct. Mere **solicitation**, however, to commit a crime is not inducement. Inducement requires a showing of at least persuasion or mild coercion.

Self-defense

As a matter of political theory, the right to use force is handed over to the government via the social contract. This power to use force is entrusted to law enforcement. Thus, when force is called for to end a confrontation, people should call the police. There are times, however, when the police are not available in emergencies. In these rare instances, it is permissible for the average citizen to use force to protect themselves and others from violent victimization.

The legality of using force in **self-defense** hinges on reasonableness. Whether a use of force decision was a reasonable one will always depend on the circumstances of each individual situation. The amount of force used should be the minimum likely to repel the attack. The defense also requires that the danger be **imminent**. In other words, the use of force cannot be preemptive or retaliatory. Generally, **deadly force** can only be used to prevent loss of life. Some jurisdictions allow the use of **non-deadly force** to prevent thefts.

Intoxication

While there is some logic to the idea that being intoxicated diminishes a person's capacity to develop *mens rea*, it usually serves to enhance rather than mitigate criminal culpability. There are some jurisdictions that allow **voluntary intoxication** as a factor that mitigates culpability, such as when murder in the first degree is reduced to murder in the second degree. Involuntary intoxication is another matter. If a defendant has been given a drug without their knowledge, then a defense of **involuntary intoxication** may be available.

Mistake

It is often said, "Everybody makes mistakes." The law recognizes this, and **mistake** can sometimes be a defense to a criminal charge. Mistakes made because the situation was not really the way the person thought it was are known as **mistakes of fact**. These can be a criminal defense. Mistakes as to matters of law (**mistakes of law**) can never be used as a criminal defense. There is a presumption in American law that everyone knows the criminal law. This may seem like a preposterous assumption, but consider the alternative. If a defendant could mount a defense by claiming that he or she did not know the act was criminal, then everyone could commit every crime at least once and get away with it by claiming that they did not know. For this reason, the law has to presume that everybody knows the law.

Necessity

The defense of **necessity** is based on the idea that it is sometimes necessary to choose one evil to prevent another, such as when property is destroyed to save lives. The necessity defense is sometimes referred to as the **lesser of two evils** defense because the evil that he actor seeks to prevent must be a greater harm that the evil that he or she does to prevent it. In most jurisdictions, the defense will not be available if the person created the danger they were avoiding.

Duress

Duress, sometimes known as **coercion**, means that the actor did the criminal act because they were forced to do so by another person by means of a threat. The idea is that while the actor commits the *actus reus* of the offense, the *mens rea* element, the criminal intent, was that of the person that coerced the actor to commit the crime. The effect of a successful duress defense is a matter of state law, so may be different in different jurisdictions. Most jurisdictions require that the actor have no part in becoming involved in the situation.

Key Terms

Coercion, Deadly Force, Duress, Entrapment, Excuse, Imminent Danger, Insanity Defense, Involuntary Intoxication, Irresistible Impulse Test, Justification, Lesser of Two Evils Defense, Mistake Defense, Mistake of Fact, Mistake of Law, M'Naghten Rule, Necessity Defense, Non-deadly Force, Not Guilty By Reason of Insanity, *Parsons v. State* (1887), Self-defense, Solicitation, Substantial Capacity Test, Voluntary Intoxication

Section 3.5: Substantive Offenses

Learning Objectives

After completing this section, you should be able to:

3.5(a) Compare and contrast to common law elements of murder with the modern statutory definition provided by the Model Penal Code.
3.5(b) Differentiate between an assault and a battery.
3.5(c) Describe the evolution of the law defining the offense of rape, including the idea of rape shield laws.
3.5(d) Compare and contrast the common law definition of arson with the modern statutory definition provided by the Model Penal Code.
3.5(e) Compare and contrast the elements of robbery with the elements of burglary.

Introduction

Unlike the social scientific definitions of crime that essentially consider only the act, legal definitions of crimes are more complex. An important aspect of understanding these legal definitions is understanding the common elements that constitute each crime. Once the essential elements of crimes are understood, it is a relatively easy matter to consider the elements that must be proven in court to obtain a conviction. Recall that each element of the crime must be proven beyond a reasonable doubt.

Murder

At common law, **murder** was defined as killing another human being with malice aforethought. Malice aforethought is a legal term of art that goes beyond the obvious meaning of the two terms. The term *malice* means the intention to do evil. It is sometimes defined as "ill will." *Aforethought* means thought about or planned beforehand. If we put the two together, it suggests that the plan to cause harm was premeditated. This "murder with intent to kill" is one legal way to look at it, but at common law, malice aforethought could be satisfied in other ways. An alternative was a murder committed when the intent was only to cause **grievous bodily harm**. In addition, a person was guilty of murder if someone else was killed in the while committing a felony. This is known as the **felony murder rule**.

Most murders require the specific intent to harm the person that dies. When someone does something that kills somebody, but there was no specific target, then there is a **depraved heart murder.** A classic example of this is firing a rifle into a passenger train car. No specific victim was intended, but it was highly likely that someone would die.

While there are some differences in these common law classifications of murder and the modern statutory classifications, their underlying prohibitions are the same. The Model Penal Code, for example, prohibits purposefully or knowingly killing another human being. This functions in a nearly identical way to the common law rule against intentional murder. The Model Penal Code punishes killings that come from "extreme recklessness" in a way that mimics the depraved heart murder of common law. The Model Penal Code creates a **rebuttable presumption** that a killing committed during the commission of certain felonies shows extreme recklessness. This provision mimics the felony murder rule in function.

Assault and Battery

In everyday language, **assault** and **battery** are used interchangeably. In many jurisdictions, however, they are two distinct offenses. An assault is an act that creates an imminent fear that the victim will be harmed, but no actual harm occurs. In other words, an assault is a threat of force. A battery is a physical act that results in some actual harm to the victim. Some jurisdictions include any offensive touching in the definition of battery. Many jurisdictions define an unwanted touching of the sexual organs of another person as a **sexual battery**. Note that in most cases, the assault is a lesser-included offense of the battery. That means that in jurisdictions that have both assault and battery statutes, both offenses cannot be charged against the same person for the same act.

Rape

Rape is a crime that has evolved dramatically over time. At common law, rape was defined as *the unlawful carnal knowledge of a female without her consent*. In this common law context, the term unlawful means that law did not authorize the act. Historically, this precluded applying the rape law to a husband who forced his wife to have sex (now known as **marital rape**). *Carnal knowledge* is synonymous with *sexual intercourse*. Thus, the law was very specific; many violent sexual acts (such as those perpetrated against men) did not fit the legal definition of rape.

Historically, rape has been a very difficult crime for the state to prove. The most difficult element to prove in court tends to be the fact that the woman did not consent to the act. Many jurisdictions required that the victim offer forceful resistance to the perpetrator. In addition, many required that the victim be of "previously chaste character." Defense attorneys would use this requirement to attack the victim on the witness stand, increasing the trauma of an already traumatic event. Most states have now passed what are known as **rape shield laws**. These are laws designed to protect victims of rape from further trauma. Most of these laws prohibit the introduction of evidence about the victim's past sexual history and reputation.

The changing legal climate of rape law has influenced the definition used by the FBI's Uniform Crime Reports program. The traditional UCR definition was "The carnal knowledge of a female forcibly and against her will." Many agencies interpreted this definition as excluding a long list of sex offenses that are criminal in most jurisdictions, such as offenses involving oral or anal penetration, penetration with objects, and rapes of males. The new Summary definition of Rape is: "Penetration, no matter how slight, of the vagina or anus with any body part or object, or oral penetration by a sex organ of another person, without the consent of the victim." This language is very similar to that of the Model Penal Code's rape statute.

Arson

Arson has always been considered a very serious crime. At various times, the penalty under the common law was death by burning. **Common law arson** was very narrowly defined as the *malicious burning of the dwelling of another*. In the common law context, a malicious burning was one where the perpetrator had criminal intent. The *burning* requirement did not mean that the dwelling had to be completely consumed by the fire. Smoke and blackening were generally considered to be insufficient; some part of the structure (albeit a very small amount) must be destroyed by the fire.

Modern statutory definitions have tended to expand on what is covered by arson. Today, most all structures will qualify. Many states include the burning of any valuable property in the definition of arson, setting the penalty based on the value of the property destroyed. The model penal code requires that the arsonist have the purpose of destroying another person's building or other structure.

Robbery

Robbery is the taking of the property of another by the use of force or threat of force. Because of the force involved, most jurisdictions classify robbery as a crime against persons rather than a property crime. For this reason, some force is required for a theft of property to amount to a robbery. Purse snatching, for example, does not constitute a robbery in most jurisdictions because the only force involved was the amount necessary to acquire possession of the property. Many states divide robbery into categories based on the seriousness of the offense. The use of a weapon, especially a firearm, often elevates the crime to aggravated robbery or first-degree robbery, depending on the jurisdiction. Most robbery statutes are state laws, but some robberies, notably those that affect interstate commerce or the currency, are matters of federal law.

Burglary

At common law, **burglary** required that the crime take place in the dwelling house of another at night. Most states have greatly broadened this requirement to include any structure at any time of day. Many jurisdictions draw a distinction between residential burglary and commercial burglary, with the penalty being more severe for residential burglary. Burglary is much more serious than a mere theft of property because it involves the home, which is sacred under the common law tradition, and the risk of violence is high.

Most modern statutes require a breaking and entering into the home or other structure of another person with the intent to commit a crime therein. Under most circumstances, the crime will be a theft. Other offenses contemplated within the structure, such as rape, can also meet the requirements for burglary.

Classification of Juvenile Behaviors

Recall that there is a separate juvenile system that is operated in parallel with the adult system. The special treatment of juveniles extends into the criminal law along with other aspects of the criminal justice system. The OJJDP estimates that about 1.3 million juveniles were arrested in 2013, continuing a downward trend in the number of persons under the age of 18 arrested each year. Only about 61,000 if these were offenses listed on the Violent Crime Index. The remaining offenses were property crimes and nonviolent offenses. Some of these were status offenses, such as **truancy**, curfew violations, and running away.

The vast majority of these arrests were for nonviolent crimes. About 5% were for minor offenses, such as **truancy**, running away, or curfew violations. Because the juvenile justice system is different that the adult criminal justice system, a different classification scheme has been developed to describe children. There are three basic categories of youths under the jurisdiction of the Juvenile Courts.

Delinquents

Delinquents are youths who commit acts that would be considered as criminal of the same act were committed by an adult. This classification includes both misdemeanors and felonies.

Status Offenders

Status offenders are youths who commit acts that would not be defined as criminal if committed by an adult, but are only taken notice of *because* of the juvenile's age (e.g., truancy, running away from home, and curfew violations).

Dependent and Neglected Children

Dependent and neglected children are youths who are disadvantaged in some way and in need of support and supervision.

Key Terms

Arson, Assault, Battery, Burglary, Carnal Knowledge, Commercial Burglary, Common Law Arson, Delinquents, Dependent and Neglected Children, Depraved Heart Murder, Dwelling House, Felony Murder Rule, Grievous Bodily Harm, Lesser-included Offense, Marital Rape, Murder, Rape, Rape Shield Laws, Rebuttable Presumption, Residential Burglary, Robbery, Sexual Battery, Status Offenders, Status Offenses, Truancy

Chapter 4: Law Enforcement

For as long as there have been historical records, there has been a need to protect societies from rogue members that would victimize other members of society and violate social norms. For most of human history, the enforcement of social norms (and later laws) fell on the entire group. In other words, people policed themselves. It was not until the Industrial Revolution that people began to turn this task over to the uniformed law enforcement professionals we know as police today.

The police are very powerful members of modern society. They have the authority to deprive members of our society of their liberty. They have a monopoly on the lawful use of force and often use that authority to make arrests and to protect life and property. Problems arise when the public perceives that this power has been abused rather than prudently and lawfully used. Perhaps the biggest issue facing law enforcement today is the public perception that law enforcement officers often abuse their authority when they decide to use force against minorities.

Section 4.1: Early History of Policing

Learning Objectives

After completing this section, you should be able to:

4.1(a) Describe how policing was done in the earliest human societies.
4.1(b) Name and provide the origin of the earliest written codes of law.
4.1(c) Describe the major elements of the mutual pledge system.
4.1(d) Describe the major elements of the watch and ward system.
4.1(e) Sketch the early history of the London Metropolitan Police and explain the impact of Robert Peel's innovations on policing in America.
4.1(f) Describe the political era of policing in America and its associated problems.
4.2(g) Describe the key reformers and the key reforms of the reform era.

Introduction

The legal system of the United States traces its roots back to the common law of England. The enforcement of those ancient laws was the responsibility of a criminal justice system that grew and evolved over a protracted period. The protections against the abuse of police power that Americans enjoy today have their roots in English constitutional documents such as the *Magna Carta*. Legally limited police authority and a decentralized organizational structure are two of the most important features of modern American policing attributable to its English colonial past.

Ancient Policing

Historians and anthropologists regard the earliest system of law enforcement as **kin policing**. In this primitive system, members of a clan or tribe banded together to enforce the rules of the group on rogue members. The essence of kin policing was the idea that an attack on one member of the group was tantamount to an attack on the entire group. Note that this method was extremely informal: there were no courts or written system of laws. Behavioral expectations were derived from group norms and customs.

When formal, written laws emerged, the need to enforce those laws emerged concurrently. King Hammurabi of Babylon is credited with the first written criminal code. The **Code of Hammurabi** was carved in large stones in the tenth century B.C. The codes of ancient Greece and Rome have had an influence on Western law, as has the **Mosaic Code**.

Among the earliest documented Western systems of law and law enforcement was the **mutual pledge system**. The mutual pledge system consisted of groups of ten families bound to uphold the law, bring violators to court, and keep the peace. These groups of ten families were known as **tithings**. Each tithing was governed by a **tithingman**. All men over the age of twelve were required to raise the **hue and cry** when a crime was detected, and pursue the criminal with all of the men of the tithing. A group of ten tithings was called the **hundred**, and the office of constable developed out of this organizational unit. If a criminal could not be produced in court, then the Crown could fine the entire hundred. In other words, every man was responsible for the conduct of every other man.

Hundreds were combined into administrative units known as **Shires** (or Counties), under the jurisdiction of the **shire-reeve**. The shire-reeve, whose job it was to maintain the King's peace in the Shire, was later shortened to the modern term *sheriff*. The sheriff has the power to raise all able-bodied men in the county to pursue a criminal. This power was known by the Latin phrase *posse comitatus*.

In 1066, the Normans invaded England and seized the throne. The Norman King, William the Conqueror, quickly modified the mutual pledge system to aid in the consolidation of his power. The modified system—known as the **frankpledge system**—was a tightening of the system then Normans found in place.

By the end of the thirteenth century, the constable system had developed into the system of rural law enforcement common to all of England. The office of constable was filled by yearly elections within each parish (a religious division similar to a County). The constable had the same responsibility as the tithingman, with the additional duties of being a royal officer. In urban areas, the **watch and ward** system developed along similar lines. Officers of the watch would guard the town gates at night, conduct patrols to prevent burglary, arrest strangers appearing at night, and put out fires. By the 1361 A.D., the old system had given way to constables working under justices of the peace. This system would remain in place until the industrial revolution.

Colonial America

When the early colonists set up a system of laws and law enforcement in America, they brought the common law system of England with them. In this early system, the county sheriff was the most important law enforcement official. The duties of the sheriff in those times were far more expansive than they are today. Then the sheriff collected taxes, supervised elections, and so forth. As far as law enforcement goes, the role of the sheriff in colonial America was completely reactive. If a citizen complained, the sheriff would investigate the matter. If evidence could be collected, an arrest would be made. There were no preventive efforts, and preventive patrol was not conducted.

The Rise of Modern Policing

The United States has followed a different path than many other countries. Whereas many western nations have national police forces, the United States is still very fragmented. Policing is done mostly on the local level. One term for this **decentralized**. While there are some rather abstract political advantages to a decentralized system of law enforcement, it is not without cost. Many critics call for the **amalgamation** and centralization of police forces, citing a wide variety of reasons such as preventing wasted effort and wasted resources. The decentralized nature of modern American policing stems from its roots in the English past.

In 1829, Home Secretary Robert Peel convinced the Parliament in England to pass the Metropolitan Police Act. The primary purpose of the Act was to do away with the ineffectual patchwork of policing measures then practiced in London, and establish an around the clock, uniformed police force charged with preventing disorder and crime. Peel is credited with many innovations that became standard police practice around the world. A major shift was an effort at crime prevention rather than "raising the hue and cry" after a crime was committed. In other words, the focus of policing efforts shifted from *reactive* to *proactive*. This shift meant that the new police force was tasked with preventing crime before it occurred rather than responding to it after the fact. A key element of this proactive strategy was **preventive patrol**. Police constables became known as "Bobbies" after Robert Peel. The city of London was divided up into **beats**, and the Bobbies were ordered to patrol their beats on foot. The idea was that the presence of these uniformed officers on the streets would deter crime.

The militaristic nature of most modern police forces was also one of Peel's innovations. He used a military-style organizational structure, complete with ranks like sergeant, lieutenant, and captain. While commonplace now, military-style uniforms were an innovation. Command and discipline were also conducted along military lines.

It was not long before the value of such police forces was noted by America's largest cities and the idea was selectively imported. The main element of the British model that Americans rejected was the **nationalization** of police services. Americans at the time were still fearful of strong central authority, and elected to establish police forces on a local level. While arguably more democratic, decentralized police forces organized on the local level were not nearly as well insulated from local politics as their British counterparts. Political leaders were able to exert a large amount of influence over police hiring, policymaking, and field practices.

There is some debate amongst the concerned departments as to whether Boston or New York City was the first modern police force in the United States. Boston's day watch was established in 1838, and many credit this as the first modern police force. New York City formed its police force in 1844. Most other large cities soon followed suit, and full-time, salaried officers became the norm.

Early Problems with Police

As previously mentioned, early police forces were highly political. Graft and corruption were rampant. Police ranks were filled with officers of particular ethnic groups to garner votes for particular politicians. Criminals paying off the police to ignore vice crimes was also common. Policing was more about political advantage than protecting public safety in many neighborhoods. Efforts to eliminate corruption were doomed from the start because the very politicians that had the power to end it benefited from it. This period from approximately 1940 to 1920 has become known as the **political era** of policing due to these political ties.

The Reform Era

The end of the 19th century saw progressive thinkers attempt to reform the police. Progressivism was a broadly focused political and social movement of the day, and the police were swept up in this wave of progress, improvement, and reform. The status quo of policing would not withstand its momentum. A primary objective of the police reformers of this era was to reduce substantially the power of local politicians over the police.

An important reform was the institution of **civil service**. The aim of civil service was to make selection and promotion decisions based on merit and testing rather than by the corrupt system of political patronage of the previous era. Within police circles, the progressive movement spawned an interest in the professionalization of policing. Model professional police departments would be highly efficient, separated from political influence, and staffed by experts.

One of the most notable police reformers and champions of police professionalism was the Chief of police in Berkeley, California from 1909 to 1932. August Vollmer defined police professionalism in terms of effective crime control, educated officers, and nonpolitical public service. Like Peel a generation before, Vollmer is known for many firsts in policing. He was the first to develop an academic degree program in law enforcement in an era long before the establishment of criminal justice as a field of study in American universities. His agency was among the first to use forensic science to aid investigations, and among the first to use automobiles. His agency was among the first to establish a code of ethics, which prohibited the acceptance of gratuities and favors by officers.

One of Vollmer's students, O. W. Wilson is known for introducing the concepts of scientific management into policing and increasing efficiency. Wilson was one of the first police administrators to advocate single officer patrols. Later in his career he became a professor at the University of California at Berkeley, and was known as America's foremost expert on police administration.

Key Terms

Amalgamation, August Vollmer, Beat, Civil Service, Code of Hammurabi, Decentralized, Frankpledge System, Hue and Cry, Hundred, Kin Policing, Magna Carta, Mosaic Code, Mutual Pledge System, Nationalization, O. W. Wilson, Parish, Political Era, Posse Comitatus, Preventive Patrol, Proactive, Reactive, Reform Era, Shire, Shire-reeve, Tithing, Tithingman, Watch and Ward

Section 4.2: The Structure and Nature of Policing

Learning Objectives

After completing this section, you should be able to:

4.2(a)   List and describe the three levels of law enforcement in the United States today.
4.2(b)   List and describe the major functions of police in the United States today.
4.2(c)   Identify Wilson's three styles of policing, and discuss the differences between them.
4.2(d)   Describe the mission of America's premier federal law enforcement agencies.
4.2(e)   Explain why police departments in America are often described as quasi-military organizations.
4.2(f)   Explain why police departments in America are often described as bureaucratic organizations.

Introduction

Perhaps the most enduring myth of criminal justice is the actual role of the police officer in our society. From early television programs such as *Dragnet* up to today's most compelling crime dramas, cops live a life full of danger, always encountering dangerous fugitives, serial killers, and other villains that must be outwitted, outfought, and outgunned. Of course, danger is part of the police job. It is, however, a mistake to assume that this is the only job that the police do. Most of what the police do on a daily basis is to deal with what Herman Goldstein (1990) called "the residual problems of society."

Police Functions

Movies and television have defined the role of the police in the popular imagination as that of "crime fighter." In reality, catching "bad guys" and investigating crimes is only a small fraction of what the police are called upon to do every day. In reality, calls for social services order maintenance tasks are far more common.

A large fraction of the average police officer's shift is spent helping people with problems that have nothing to do with apprehending felons. People get hurt in automobile accidents, and police officers are there to render aid. People lose things ranging from cell phones to children and expect the police to help find them. Some authors estimate that well over fifty percent of calls for police services involve these kinds of social service tasks. By comparison, these same authors estimate that only about 20% of calls for police services relate to crime.

Many law enforcement activities have to do with keeping society running smoothly. These things—such as traffic control, crowd control, and moving prostitutes off the streets—are frequently referred to as "order maintenance" activities. A key difference between law enforcement and order maintenance is that order maintenance activities are not generally concerned with the letter of the law, but rather keeping the peace. Arrest is always an option when an officer is trying to preserve the peace, but less formal solutions are far more commonly employed. For example, when the driver of a stopped car that is blocking traffic complies with an officer's request to move along, no citation is issued.

The American Bar Association (1986), in a document called *Standards Relating to the Urban Police Function*, lists 11 responsibilities of the police:

(a) identify criminal offenders and criminal activity and, where appropriate, to apprehend offenders and participate in subsequent court proceedings;
(b) reduce the opportunities for the commission of some crimes through preventive patrol and other measures;

(c) aid individuals who are in danger of physical harm;

(d) protect constitutional guarantees;

(e) facilitate the movement of people and vehicles;

(f) assist those who cannot care for themselves;

(g) resolve conflict;

(h) identify problems that are potentially serious law enforcement or governmental problems;

(i) create and maintain a feeling of security in the community;

(j) promote and preserve civil order; and

(k) provide other services on an emergency basis.

The last element in this list provides the primary reason why the police are called upon to deal with the "residual problems" of society: There is no one else available twenty-four hours a day, seven days a week.

Another key factor that makes the police unique is what some authors have referred to as a "monopoly on the use of force." The authorization to use force means that the police hold a position of great power within our society, and this translates into a great responsibility to use that force ethically.

Despite all of that power, there is a trend among policing experts to call for broad discretion for police officers. Officers who have their hands bound by excessive policies and procedures cannot solve community problems. Officers must have the authority to identify community problems, tailor solutions to those problems, and implement those solutions. Even in departments where community policing is not the dominant paradigm, officers still have a great deal of discretion. For example, officers decide who gets a warning and who gets a citation. Officers decide who is arrested. Officers decide when force is necessary. Of course, some obvious factors are used by officers when making a discretionary decision. The seriousness of a crime and the strength of evidence, for example, are factors in the decision to make or not make an arrest. Personal factors also come into play; researchers discovered long ago that the demeanor of the suspect plays an important role in the decision to arrest. Respectful and deferential citizens are less likely to be arrested than rude or belligerent ones.

The Structure of Policing in America

Local police departments make up more than two-thirds of the 18,000 state and local law enforcement agencies in the United States. The Bureau of Justice Statistics (BJS) defines a local police department is a general purpose law enforcement agency, other than a sheriff's office, that is operated by a unit of local government such as a town, city, township, or county. Tribal police are classified as local police BJS statistics. In 2008, local police departments had about 593,000 full-time employees, including 461,000 sworn officers. About 60% of all state and local sworn personnel were local police officers.

Federal Law Enforcement Agencies

The Federal Bureau of Investigation (FBI): The FBI is housed within the United States Department of Justice. The FBI is rather unique in that it has both law enforcement and national security concerns as part of its mission. As the FBI's *Mission Statement* puts it, they are a "... national security organization with both intelligence and law enforcement responsibilities..." The *Mission Statement* further explains, "The mission of the FBI is to protect and defend the United States against terrorist and foreign intelligence threats, to uphold and enforce the criminal laws of the United States, and to provide leadership and criminal justice services to federal, state, municipal, and international agencies and partners." The FBI employs 13,785 special agents and 22,117 support professionals, such as intelligence analysts, language specialists, scientists, information technology specialists, and other professionals (FBI, 2013).

The Bureau of Alcohol, Tobacco, and Firearms (ATF): The ATF has a reputation for dealing with illegal firearms. Its mission is rather broader in reality. Housed within the United States Department of Justice, the ATF protects American communities from violent criminals, criminal organizations, the illegal use and trafficking of firearms, the illegal use and storage of explosives, acts of arson and bombings, acts of terrorism, and the illegal diversion of alcohol and tobacco products (ATF, 2013).

The Drug Enforcement Administration (DEA): "The mission of the Drug Enforcement Administration (DEA) is to enforce the controlled substances laws and regulations of the United States and bring to the criminal and civil justice system of the United States, or any other competent jurisdiction, those organizations and principal members of organizations, involved in the growing, manufacture, or distribution of controlled substances appearing in or destined for illicit traffic in the United States; and to recommend and support non-enforcement programs aimed at reducing the availability of illicit controlled substances on the domestic and international markets" (DEA, 2013).

The U.S. Marshals Service: "The U.S. Marshals Service (USMS) is the nation's oldest and most versatile federal law enforcement agency. Federal Marshals have served the country since 1789, often times in unseen but critical ways. The USMS is the enforcement arm of the federal courts, and as such, it is involved in virtually every federal law enforcement initiative. Presidentially appointed U.S. Marshals direct the activities of 94 districts — one for each federal judicial district. More than 3,950 Deputy Marshals and Criminal Investigators form the backbone of the agency. Among their many duties, they apprehend more than half of all federal fugitives, protect the federal judiciary, operate the Witness Security Program, transport federal prisoners, conduct body searches, enforce court orders and Attorney General orders involving civil disturbances and acts of terrorism, execute civil and criminal processes, and seize property acquired by criminals through illegal activities."

The Secret Service: The United States Secret Service began as an agency dedicated to the investigation of crimes related to the Treasury, and then evolved into the United States' most recognized protection agency. The Secret Service was a part of the Department of the Treasury until March 1, 2003, when it became a part of the Department of Homeland Security. "The mission of the United States Secret Service is to safeguard the nation's financial infrastructure and payment systems to preserve the integrity of the economy, and to protect national leaders, visiting heads of state and government, designated sites and National Special Security Events."

The Citizenship and Immigration Service (USCIS): U.S. Citizenship and Immigration Services is the government agency that oversees lawful immigration to the United States. "USCIS will secure America's promise as a nation of immigrants by providing accurate and useful information to our customers, granting immigration and citizenship benefits, promoting an awareness and understanding of citizenship, and ensuring the integrity of our immigration system. The agency is composed of over 19,000 government employees and contractors of USCIS working at 223 offices across the world.

Transportation Security Administration (TSA). The primary mission of the TSA is to protect travelers and interstate commerce. TSA uses a risk-based strategy and works closely with transportation, law enforcement, and intelligence communities to set the standard for excellence in transportation security.

State Law Enforcement Agencies

Every state in the United States has a state-level police force with the exception of Hawaii. The largest of these state-level agencies is the California Highway Patrol.

One of the major purposes of the state police in most jurisdictions is to provide patrol services, especially on remote highways where local law enforcement is sparse. State police are often called upon to aid local law enforcement in criminal investigations that are complex or cross local jurisdictional lines. Often they are responsible for maintaining centralized criminal records for the state, operating crime labs, and training local officers.

Local Law Enforcement Agencies

In the United States today, there is a Hollywood generated myth that the federal government does major fraction of the law enforcement workload. This is not true. The vast majority of criminal cases are generated by local agencies such as sheriffs' departments and local police departments.

Sheriffs' Offices

According to the BJS (Burch, 20012), an estimated 3,012 sheriffs' offices performing law enforcement functions in the United States employed 369,084 sworn and civilian personnel. Sheriffs' offices represented approximately a fifth of the estimated 15,600 general-purpose law enforcement agencies operating in the United States. Although sheriffs' offices may have countywide responsibilities related to jail operation, process serving, and court security, their law enforcement jurisdictions typically exclude county areas served by a local police department. In certain counties, municipalities contract with the sheriffs' office for law enforcement services. Large agencies (employing 100 or more sworn personnel) represented about 12% of all sheriffs' offices but employed nearly two-thirds (65%) of all full-time sworn personnel.

Local Police Departments

About half of local police departments employed fewer than 10 sworn personnel, and about three-fourths served a population of less than 10,000. In 2007, about 1 in 8 local police officers were women, compared to 1 in 13 in 1987. About 1 in 4 officers were members of a racial or ethnic minority in 2007, compared to 1 in 6 officers in 1987. In 2007, more than 4 in 5 local police officers were employed by a department that used physical agility tests (86%) and written aptitude tests (82%) in the hiring process, and more than 3 in 5 by one that used personality inventories (66%).

Wilson's Police Management Styles

James Wilson (not to be confused with O. W. Wilson), identified three police management styles:

The **watchman style** of management focuses on order maintenance. Officers often ignore minor violations of the law, unless the violation constitutes a breach of the peace. Minor violations and disputes between citizens are largely handled in an informal way.

The **legalistic style** tends to handle matters formally. In other words, policing is done "by the book." The administrative emphasis is on reducing line officer discretion and effecting unvarying, impartial arrests for all violations.

The **service style** emphasizes community service above enforcing the law. Arrest is often seen as a last resort, used only when referrals to social service organizations and agencies will be ineffectual.

Quasi-military Features

As one of Peel's major innovations, the organization of police agencies along military lines has withstood the test of time. Police officers in most jurisdictions still wear uniforms, carry weapons, and have military ranks. These ranks suggest a military style, authoritarian command structure where orders come down from the top. This militaristic view of the police is encouraged by political rhetoric such as the "war on crime" and the "war on drugs." While most America citizens take this quasi-military organization for granted, there are those that see it as a problem.

Detractors of the quasi-military organization of America's police forces suggest that by subscribing to the idea that they are engaged in a war, police officers will be tempted to slip into the mentality that "all is fair in war." They fear that a warfare mentality will lead to an "ends justify the means" mentality that results in unethical police conduct such as perjury, brutality, and other abuses of power. Other critics feel that the militaristic look of police uniforms, especially BDUs and SWAT gear, serve to intimidate the public.

The Police Bureaucracy

Modern American Police agencies are characterized by a **bureaucratic** structure. The positive aspects of bureaucratic organizations revolve around competence and clarity. Tasks and duties are specialized, qualifications for different positions are carefully and clearly defined, everyone acts according to rules and regulations, and authority exists within a clearly defined hierarchy. The idea of bureaucracy is to improve efficiency and effectiveness. The downside to this is often a lack of flexibility, being bogged down in "red tape," and ignoring the human element of serving the community.

Key Terms

American Bar Association, BDU, Bureau of Alcohol, Tobacco, and Firearms (ATF), Citizenship and Immigration Service (USCIS), Drug Enforcement Administration (DEA), Federal Bureau of Investigation (FBI), James Wilson, Legalistic Style, Local Police Department, Order Maintenance, Quasi-Military Organization, Residual Problems of Society, Secret Service, Service Style, SWAT, Sworn Officer, Transportation Security Administration (TSA), Tribal Police, U.S. Marshals Service (USMS), Watchman Style

Section 4.3: Police Methods

Learning Objectives

After completing this section, you should be able to:

4.3(a)   Explain why the patrol division is referred to as the "backbone" of policing.
4.3(b)   Describe the Kansas City Preventive Patrol Experiment, and its implications for law enforcement practice.
4.3(c)   Compare and contrast proactive policing with reactive policing.
4.3(d)   Describe the origins and methods of Problem-oriented Policing.
4.3(e)   Define and describe the major components of Community-oriented Policing.

Introduction

For most of its history in America, the work of the patrol officer and the investigator constituted the vast majority of police work. Uniformed officers patrolled the streets of America's cities, serving as a highly visible deterrent to crime and attempting to catch criminals in the act. If patrol failed, the investigator's job was to follow up, solving crimes by questioning victims, witnesses, and suspects. Only since the 1960s has empirical research highlighted the limits of both preventive patrol and criminal investigations in dealing with America's crime problem. It was not until the early 1990s that this research spawned a new wave of police reform aimed at proactive policing strategies. These proactive strategies meant that police efforts would shift (at least to some degree) from responding to calls for service to initiating action.

Patrol

Patrol is often called the "backbone" of the police department, and for good reason. Patrol consumes most of the average police department's resources. The basic philosophy and strategy of preventive patrol has not changed from Peel's time: the patrol officer makes circuits through a specified area, often called a beat. During Peel's time, most patrols were done on foot, with the occasional horse patrol. Technology ushered in the automobile, and modern police forces take full advantage of the benefits offered by cars. The most important of these advantages is the area that a single officer can cover. Automobile patrol officers can cover much wider beat areas than officers on foot. The bottom line is that because an officer in a car can cover a much wider geographic area, departments need fewer officers. This translates into huge savings. Automobile patrol is much cheaper than foot patrol.

The effectiveness of patrol operations within a department is usually judged by three major functions. These include answering calls for service, deterring crime by a highly visible police presence, and investigating suspicious circumstances. Of these three major functions of patrol, crime deterrence is the most controversial. The historical assumption, stemming from Peel's day, was that a highly visible officer patrolling a beat would serve as a deterrent to would-be criminals. Research evidence since the 1970s has supported the idea that random preventive patrol has very little if any impact on crime.

The Kansas City Preventive Patrol Experiment

In the 1970s, criminal justice researchers began to question the underlying assumption of preventive patrol. They designed an experiment to find out of preventive patrol reduced crime and made citizens feel safe from crime. They also wondered about patrol strength. In other words, did the number of officers on patrol in a given area have an impact on both actual crime and citizens' perceptions of crime?

The researchers' experiment was conducted in conjunction with the Kansas City, Missouri police department. The department divided the city's 15 beat areas into 3 groups. As with any good experiment, the experimenters needed a control group. To serve this purpose, one cluster of 5 beats made no changes in the amount of patrol officers working in the area. In a second area, the police withdrew all preventive patrol and served a completely reactive role. They entered this "reactive" area only when calls for service were received. In the third area, they raised preventive patrol to four times the normal level. If the conventional wisdom about the effectiveness of preventive patrol held true, then the experimenters should observe a higher crime rate in the reactive area, no change in the crime rate in the control area, and a drop in the intensified patrol area.

What the researchers found staggered the world of policing: There was almost no difference in actual crime or citizens fear of crime. Citizen's opinions about how good a job the police were doing did not change. It seemed that law-abiding citizens and criminals alike simply did not notice the changes. As one would expect, this caused a flurry of opinions to come out regarding the interpretation of these findings. Some argued that the findings must be wrong, and that preventive patrol was and always had been a good thing. Others argued that patrol was just a bad idea and that the police should focus on different things. Many stood the middle ground, focusing on making patrol more effective by changing the way it was done. One of the few things that almost all commentators agreed on was that just pouring more officers out on the street would have little impact on crime. What was needed was a fundamental change.

The Proactive Paradigm Shift

While the research evidence seems to indicate that the mere presence of uniformed officers in an area does little to deter crime, the same cannot be said of more aggressive patrol strategies. Proactive patrol operations shift from random to targeted. Specific types of offenders, specific places, and specific types of victims can be considered. Myriad tactics fall under this general philosophy. Undercover operations, the use of informants, using decoys, saturating problem areas, and frequent patrols of "hot spots" are just a few examples.

An important argument in how to better utilize patrol is that random patrols do not work well because crime is not a random phenomenon. While it may seem fair, giving every neighborhood in a city an equal amount of police time and resources is horribly inefficient. A smarter use of resources is to concentrate police resources in high crime areas, and limit resources in areas that experience very little crime. Research evidence suggests that this strategy does indeed have a positive impact on crime. Researchers found that the 911 system received a heavy amount of calls for service from a small number of locations. Brief periods of intensive patrolling in those high crime areas effectively reduced robberies and other crimes.

Other strategies, such as those used in the **San Diego Field Interrogation Study**, have shown that aggressively interrogating suspicious persons can lead to a reduction in both violent crime and disorder. The New York City Street Crimes Unit has had success using decoys to apprehend repeat offenders. By having an undercover officer play a "perfect victim," officers were able to increase dramatically arrests of muggers.

Problem-oriented Policing

The traditional model of policing in the United States was decidedly *reactive* in nature. The primary methods used by police were preventive patrols and retroactive investigations. Early efforts at innovation were designed to be proactive, but they focused on the deterrence of crime through a limited "toolbox" of arrests, summons, and citations. Recent decades have seen a shift in focus, due in large part to the confluence of two major developments in how both practitioners and academics viewed policing. The first was **Problem-Oriented Policing (POP)**, and the other was a broader philosophy that would include POP, known as **Community-Oriented Policing (COP)**.

Problem-oriented policing began with a seminar article published by Herman Goldstein in 1979. Goldstein essentially suggested that the basic, most fundamental job of the police was to deal with community problems. To do this job effectively, the police needed to develop a much larger toolbox, and a much more sophisticated method of detecting, analyzing, and ultimately solving these problems. This seminal article led to an explosion of interest and publication in the emerging field of problem-oriented policing. The research suggested something extraordinary about POP: it actually worked (see Braga, 2008 for a review of these studies).

A major tool in the analysis of community problems is the ***Problem Analysis Triangle***. The idea of the crime triangle is to depict graphically depict the interaction between the features of the victim, the features of the location, and the features of the offender. As Spelman and Eck (1989) point out, 10% of crime victims are involved in up to 40% of victimizations, 10% of offenders are involved in 50% of crimes, and about 10% of addresses are the location for about 60% of crimes. This suggests that a focus on a few high volume victims, offenders, and locations can maximize the impact of scarce police resources.

To understand the problem-solving process, it is helpful to consider what is meant by "problem." To understand the scope of problems of interest to police, it is helpful to consider the police mission. Under the professional model of policing, the focus was almost entirely on "catching bad guys." Other duties were often considered outside the prevue of "real police work." Goldstein suggests the following list of major police goals:

1. to prevent and control conduct threatening to life and property (including serious crime);
2. to aid crime victims and protect people in danger of physical harm;
3. to protect constitutional guarantees, such as the right to free speech and assembly;
4. to facilitate the movement of people and vehicles;
5. to assist those who cannot care for themselves, including the intoxicated, the addicted, the mentally ill, the physically disabled, the elderly, and the young;
6. to resolve conflict between individuals, between groups, or between citizens and their government;
7. to identify problems that have the potential for becoming more serious for individuals, the police or the government; and
8. to create and maintain a feeling of security in the community

Community-oriented Policing

Community policing is a philosophy that promotes organizational strategies that support the systematic use of partnerships and problem-solving techniques to proactively address the immediate conditions that give rise to public safety issues such as crime, social disorder, and fear of crime. A dramatic departure from traditional policing is the idea of collaborative partnerships. These partnerships are between police agencies and the individuals and organizations they serve. These partnerships are designed to develop solutions to problems and increase trust in police. To accomplish these goals, important changes must be made within departments. There must be a realignment of organizational management, structure, personnel, and information systems to support community partnerships and proactive problem solving.

Community policing recognizes that the idea of a small band of officers, no matter how well intentioned and well trained, can solve all of the crime, delinquency, and disorder problems in a society as vast and complex as that of the United States. Rarely can solve public safety problems alone. Community policing encourages interactive partnerships with relevant **stakeholders**. The range of potential partners is large, and these partnerships can be used to accomplish the two interrelated goals of developing solutions to problems through collaborative problem solving and improving public trust. A fundamental principle of community policing is that "The public should play a role in prioritizing and addressing public safety problems" (COPS Office, 2014, p. 4).

Partnerships

Police departments can partner with a number of other government agencies to identify community concerns and offer alternative solutions. Examples of agencies include legislative bodies, prosecutors, probation and parole, public works departments, neighboring law enforcement agencies, health and human services, child support services, ordinance enforcement, and schools. In addition, people who live, work, or otherwise have an interest in the community—volunteers, activists, formal and informal community leaders, residents, visitors and tourists, and commuters—are a valuable resource for identifying community concerns. These diverse members of the community can be engaged in achieving specific goals at town hall meetings, neighborhood association meetings, decentralized offices and storefronts in the community, and team beat assignments. Community-based organizations that provide services to the community and advocate on its behalf can be powerful partners. These groups often work with or are composed of individuals who share common interests and can include such entities as victims groups, service clubs, support groups, issue groups, advocacy groups, community development corporations, and the faith community.

For-profit businesses also have a great stake in the health of the community and can be key partners because they often bring considerable resources to bear in addressing problems of mutual concern. Businesses can help identify problems and provide resources for responses, often including their own security technology and community outreach. The local chamber of commerce and visitor centers can also assist in disseminating information about police and business partnerships and initiatives, and crime prevention practices. The media represent a powerful mechanism by which to communicate with the community. They can assist with publicizing community concerns and available solutions, such as services from government or community agencies or new laws or codes that will be enforced. In addition, the media can have a significant impact on public perceptions of the police, crime problems, and fear of crime.

Organizational Change

The community policing philosophy focuses on the way that departments are organized and managed and how the infrastructure can be changed to support the philosophical shift behind community policing. It encourages the application of modern management practices to increase efficiency and effectiveness. Community policing emphasizes changes in organizational structures to institutionalize its adoption and infuse it throughout the entire department, including the way it is managed and organized, its personnel, and its technology. Under the community policing model, police management infuses community policing ideals throughout the agency by making a number of critical changes in climate and culture, leadership, formal labor relations, decentralized decision making and accountability, strategic planning, policing and procedures, organizational evaluations, and increased transparency. Changing the climate and culture means supporting a proactive orientation that values systematic problem solving and partnerships. Formal organizational changes should support the informal networks and communication that take place within agencies to support this orientation.

Line Officer Buy-In

If community policing is going to be effective, **police unions** and similar forms of organized labor must be a part of the process and function as partners in the adoption of the community policing philosophy. Including labor groups in agency changes can ensure support for the changes that are imperative to community policing implementation. Experience has shown that departments that try to implement community policing without line officer support will almost certainly fail.

Key Terms

Automobile Patrol, Community Oriented Policing (COP), Community Policing, Control Group, Foot Patrol, Herman Goldstein, Hot Spot, Investigator, Kansas City Preventive Patrol Experiment, Line Officer, Police Union, Problem Analysis Triangle, Problem Oriented Policing (POP), San Diego Field Interrogation Study, Stakeholder, Town Hall Meeting

Section 4.4: Investigations and Specialized Units

Learning Objectives

After completing this section, you should be able to:

4.4(a)　Describe the basic duties of criminal investigators.
4.4(b)　Describe the investigative functions of patrol officers.
4.4(c)　Describe factors that influence the likelihood that a department will have specialized units.
4.4(d)　Identify the scope and nature of the problems with which domestic violence units must contend.
4.4(e)　Identify the types of crimes most commonly investigated by vice units.
4.4(f)　Describe the role of internal affairs within police departments.
4.4(g)　Describe specialized units and programs within police departments designed to prevent juvenile delinquency.

Introduction

Hollywood is responsible for several archetypical "investigators." Most of these are merely Hollywood myths that reflect nothing of what criminal investigators actually do. Perhaps the most unrealistic myth is the super sleuth that "always gets his man." In reality, police clear only about 20% of index crimes. The next most unrealistic myth is that detective live a professional life if danger and excitement. The reality is that detectives do a huge amount of boring paperwork.

What Investigators Do

Many crimes that result in arrest do so because of the "detective work" of the patrol officer that responded to the call for service. If the patrol officer cannot conclude the investigation with an arrest, the case is turned over to a criminal investigator. The primary job of the investigator is to gather information. A good detective is a jack of all trades. Much knowledge about a wide array of subjects and many skills are required. These are needed to accomplish three major functions: Conducting interviews of victims, witnesses, and suspects is perhaps the most common and most important. Second, a good investigator must have the necessary knowledge and skill to properly conduct a crime scene investigation. Finally, good detectives must have the ability to develop and maintain informants.

The research suggests that the traditional investigator's role is not that important in solving crimes. According to the National Institute of Justice (NIJ), no amount of investigation will solve many of the serious crimes that occur in America's communities. There simply is not enough evidence to go on. Other studies have found that the majority of cleared cases are cleared because of the work of patrol officers. Arrests of offenders at the scene are more common that offenders being apprehended after lengthy investigations. These findings have led to much discussion of how to improve investigations. As one would expect in an era of community policing, much of that discussion has been centered on how to make detectives a more proactive part of the police department.

The Patrol Function

While detectives are usually assigned cases in the form of a follow-up investigation, the first responder is most often a uniformed patrol officer. The early stages of a criminal investigation, often called a *preliminary investigation*, begins when dispatchers receive a call, most often through a 911 system. In many small departments, the patrol officer conducting the preliminary investigation will see the investigation through to the end. This is because either the small number of detectives available are otherwise engaged, or because the department is so small that no one is assigned permanently to investigations.

The first priority of every officer arriving at every crime scene is officer safety. The safety of the public is a close but secondary concern. This may seem counterintuitive, but wounded officers cannot protect the safety of the public and investigate crimes. Logically, officer safety must be a first priority. This is why most "active shooter" training dictates that officers first eliminate the threat before attending to the medical needs of victims. After safety issues have been adequately dealt with, the focus shifts to discovering what happened. This requires rapid assessment of the scene and the quick identification of any potential witnesses. An ongoing goal of the first responder is the security and integrity of the scene. It is vital to the preservation of evidence that absolutely no unnecessary personnel (law enforcement or civilian) enter the scene.

Once dangers have been eliminated, witnesses have been identified, and the scene has been secured, the first responder will evaluate what further (if any) investigative actions should be taken. This can mean conducting further investigations, calling in technicians, or calling in an investigator. Some crimes will fall into the jurisdiction of another agency (e.g., state police or FBI). The decision to turn an investigation over to another department or agency will usually be made at the administrative level. Patrol officers may be required to make this judgment call, however, when the public safety demands immediate action. Acts of terrorism and hazardous material spills are examples of circumstances where outside agencies should be notified immediately.

A critical aspect of all investigative activity is the meticulous keeping of accurate records. These records will take the form of departmental forms and reports, written notes, sketches, and photographs. Many patrol officers fail at this important task, mistakenly believing that crime scene documentation is a task for investigators. It must be remembered that if the job of the first responder is not done well, the chances of an investigator being able to salvage the investigation are slim.

Specialized Units

There is a strong correlation between the size of an agency's jurisdiction (in terms of population, not land area), and the existence of specialized units. That is, the bigger a city, the more specialized officers tend to be within that city's police department. The most common specialized units within American police departments are traffic units and drug enforcement units. How such units operate depends largely on departmental policy, but national priorities can also be important because the national government often funds law enforcement initiatives through grants.

Many larger departments divide investigative duties between *crimes against persons* and *crimes against property*. Each of these major categories may involve types of cases that require investigators to have special knowledge or skills. Most criminal investigators, however, are generalists. They develop a wide array of skills to perform a wide array of criminal investigations efficiently. When agencies do create specialized investigative units, they often target a specific type of crime. Domestic violence, vice, organized crimes, and sex crimes are common divisions.

Domestic Violence

Violence against intimate partners was a social problem long before that fact was widely recognized by the public. In days past, abuse of women by husbands and boyfriends was considered a "family matter," and the criminal justice system ignored most cases. Today, things have changed for the better as far as public awareness and the mandate for an appropriate police response go. The problem is still present at a level many find disturbing. Domestic violence tends to be cyclical (repeating), and the magnitude of the violence tends to increase as time goes on. In about one-third of homicide cases where the victim is female, the killer was a husband or boyfriend. Myriad acts fall under the heading of domestic violence, but the definitions used by social and behavioral scientists tend to be much broader than those used in criminal codes. Officers that subscribe to the code enforcer paradigm will often respond inappropriately or much too late.

In response to this persistent and tragic problem, many police departments have created specialized units to deal with this particular crime. These departments are in essence acknowledging that normal police tools (i.e., arrest) do not work well in domestic violence cases, and that officers need specialized training to understand the dynamics of domestic violence, and they need outside help if victims are to be assisted. In progressive departments, investigators are paired with social workers to place victim assistance on an equal footing with the criminal investigation. Aside from the obvious virtue of helping the victim escape a life of abuse, this problem-oriented approach tends to reduce dramatically the number of calls for service stemming from the same abusive relationship. Investigation and arrest alone are woefully inefficient at ending the problem of domestic violence.

Vice

The term **vice** is used to designate a category of criminal acts that are considered victimless crimes by most people. Prostitution, gambling, and drug use are common examples. Not all police departments have vice units, and specialized drug units are another common way of dealing with that particular problem. The legal codes that make these types of activities criminal are under fire from a growing number of citizens. Because the laws are unpopular, enforcement is often unpopular as well. The movement toward legalization of marijuana is currently the most commonly discussed of these issues. Several states have made the recreational use and possession of marijuana legal, contrary to the federal government's stance. For this reason, the likelihood of being arrested for possession of marijuana depends largely on the jurisdiction.

Organized Crime

The basic characteristic of *organized crime* is a group of people working together to achieve some criminal purpose. This definition includes the **mafia**, but goes far beyond it. Organized crime can be centered on supplying illegal goods and services, such as gambling and drugs. It can also include predatory crimes, such as theft, burglary, and murder. When criminal organizations are large and complex, criminal investigations become large and complex as well. Often, criminal organizations will stretch beyond state and local borders, complicating the idea of jurisdiction. Often state and local agencies become involved in these types of investigations because of the extra resources they have and their expanded jurisdiction. In addition, investigators often need special financial expertise (examining records of financial crimes) that is beyond the capability of local police. Electronic surveillance is common in the investigation of organized crime, and the technical and legal issues are often better suited to the resources and skills of state and federal investigators. The use of **confidential informants** is also common, and this adds an additional layer of legal complexity to such cases.

Internal Affairs

The question of exactly who polices the police has been controversial throughout the history of policing in America. Starting in the late 1950s, many departments set up special units within the department to investigate allegations of police misconduct. This trend continued through the 1960s, and by the end of the decade, many of America's largest police forces had **internal affairs** divisions. This development took place against a backdrop of social turmoil and the civil rights revolution that was taking place in the federal courts. The use of excessive force and corruption are perhaps the most common issues considered by internal affairs, but all violations of the law and police codes of conduct are possible targets. Internal affairs officers are usually placed outside of the usual police command structure, answering directly to the chief.

Juveniles and the Police

Crime statistics demonstrate that juveniles are responsible for a disproportionate amount of crime. This suggests that dealing with juveniles represents a disproportionate amount of police work. The juvenile impact on police workload is enhanced due to the existence of *status offenses*. Status offenses are acts that would not be criminal if done by an adult, but are prohibited for minors. Common status offenses that the police must deal with are *truancy*, running away from home, and **juvenile curfew** violations. Additionally, police are called upon to deal with juveniles in matters that are not criminal (at least on the part of the child), such as missing persons, **child abuse**, and **child neglect**. The impact of juveniles on police work is so great that many large, urban police departments have established specialized juvenile units.

Police officers encounter a wide array of problems involving juveniles; these range from dealing with status offenses to investigating serious crimes such as murder. Most police encounters with juveniles involve what policing experts refer to as **order maintenance**. Order maintenance activities include things like asking loiterers to "move along" and crowd control at large events. Research has shown that juveniles are less likely than adults to respect the police and the law, and that authoritarian rule enforcement causes resentment among juveniles. This mistrust and resentment means that policing juveniles is a difficult task.

Community policing holds promise to mend the divide between juveniles and the police. Recall that the community policing philosophy maintains that communities and police can work together to solve community problems. These problem-solving efforts can only be successful with the participation and input of all community members, including juveniles. Despite the advice of community policing experts, community policing tends to be implemented in a programmatic way. The two most common community policing programs targeting juveniles are D.A.R.E. (Drug Awareness Resistance Education) programs and the emergence of School Resource Officers (SROs) working in an increasing number of schools throughout the United States.

The D.A.R.E. program had its beginnings in Los Angeles, but quickly spread throughout the United States. In most jurisdictions, specialized juvenile officers undergo weeks of intensive training before they can become D.A.R.E. officers. This training focuses on educational material targeting mostly fifth and sixth graders. D.A.R.E. was unique in its collaborative approach between educational institutions and police departments. A common element of most D.A.R.E. programs is teaching upper elementary school children peer resistance strategies that consist of different ways of saying "no." Empirical research has shown that the programs have little long-term impact on later drug use. Despite the disappointing research findings, the programs remain quite popular and have undergone substantial revision to improve effectiveness. Perhaps the most valuable aspect of D.A.R.E. programs was demonstrating to the nation that collaboration between police and schools was possible.

An additional community policing strategy is to place uniformed police officers in the schools. This practice is more common in large urban areas, but School Resource Officers (SROs) can be found in any size school. The Omnibus Crime Control and Safe Streets Act of 1968 defines the SRO as "a career law enforcement officer, with sworn authority, deployed in community-oriented policing, and assigned by the employing police department or agency to work in collaboration with school and community-based organizations." In practice, the community policing philosophy is often not put into practice. Rather than community collaborators that build relationships and solve problems, many SROs are relegated to the function of a security guard. The U.S. Department of Justice's Office of Community Oriented Policing Services (COPS) provided $68 million that was awarded to hire and train 599 SROs in 289 communities throughout the United States. The special funding signaled a recognition that the SRO's complex role as law enforcement officer, counselor, teachers, and liaison between police, schools, and other community elements requires training beyond that traditionally offered in police academies. Research has shown that a least some SRO programs have been successful at reducing disruptive and illegal student conduct. Prosocial relationships formed between officers and students have also led to a phenomenon that community policing advocates would have predicted: School Resource Officers obtain information concerning crime in the broader community from students, improving the overall effectiveness of the police department.

Key Terms

Active Shooter, Child Abuse, Child Neglect, Clearance Rate, Confidential Informant, Crime Scene Investigation (CSI), Domestic Violence, Drug Awareness Resistance Education (D.A.R.E.), Drug Enforcement Unit, Informant, Internal Affairs, Juvenile Curfew, Mafia, Scene Integrity, School Resource Officer (SRO), Specialized Units, Traffic Unit, Vice

Section 4.5: The Legal Environment of Policing

Learning Objectives

After completing this section, you should be able to:

4.5(a)   Discuss how the Bill of Rights protects citizens from abuses by police.
4.5(b)   Define due process and explain how it has been used by the federal courts to protect citizens from abuses by local and state law enforcement.
4.5(c)   Identify the origin of and explain the function of the exclusionary rule.
4.5(d)   Explain the functioning of the fruit of the poisoned tree doctrine.
4.5(e)   Compare and contrast the everyday use of the term arrest is different that the legal meaning of the term.
4.5(f)   Summarize the landmark cases regarding searches of vehicles by police officers.
4.5(g)   Recite the Miranda warnings, and describe Supreme Court decisions that have altered Miranda since it was handed down.
4.5(g)   Recite the text of the Fourth Amendment, and explain the meaning of each clause.
4.5(h)   Recite the text of the Eighth Amendment, and explain the meaning of each clause.
4.5(i)   Discuss the issue of civil liability in policing.

Introduction

Criminal law is often used as a very general term to describe the entire body of law that is of concern to the criminal justice system. Recall that the two major parts are the substantive criminal law and the procedural criminal law. The substantive criminal law consists largely of statutes that define criminal acts. The procedural criminal law dictates how the criminal justice system should treat people. Because the police are the gatekeepers of the criminal justice system and come into contact with citizens far more often than any other component of the criminal justice system, the law of criminal procedure has more to say about how the police treat people than any other topic.

Criminal procedure, then, can be seen as a branch of law that dictates how the government investigates, prosecutes, judges, and sentences those accused of crimes. The bulk of this law is a matter of interpreting the Constitution of the United States. When it comes to how the police must treat people, the most important body of law stems from the Bill of Rights. The Supreme Court of the United States interprets the Bill of Rights, and that court has the power to establish police practice in the field. There are also state constitutions, statutes, and administrative rules that circumscribe police conduct. These are also part of the body of procedural law. Perhaps the most important laws that concern police conduct are the Fourth and Fifth Amendments of the United States Constitution.

The Fourth Amendment States that: "The right of the people to be secure in their persons, houses, papers and effects, against unreasonable searches and seizures, shall not be violated, and no Warrants shall issue, but upon probable cause, supported by Oath or affirmation, and particularly describing the place to be searched, and the persons or things to be seized."

The Fifth Amendment states that: "No person … shall be compelled in any criminal case to be a witness against himself, nor be deprived of life, liberty, or property, without due process of law."

The **Sixth Amendment** guarantees the right to a public and speedy trial, as well as the right to the assistance of counsel. The right to counsel is protected at many stages of the criminal justice process, not just at trial. Criminal defendants have the right to an attorney during custodial interrogations, for example.

The Fourteenth Amendment requires the States to observe the due process standards set forth in the federal Constitution as interpreted by federal appeals courts. This gives the federal appellate courts the authority to consider the constitutionality of acts of government agents employed by the state such as police officers and corrections officers. It also gives the high courts the authority to review the constitutionality of state statutory laws. Not all federal constitutional rights are considered to be due process rights, so some protections are not forced on the states. For example, many states do not observe the right to an indictment by a grand jury; they use a system of prosecutorial information instead.

The Right to Privacy

To understand how the Constitution of the United States limits the criminal law, it is important to consider the right to privacy. Shockingly, the term "privacy" never appears in the Constitution. Yet, over the years, the Supreme Court has said that several of the rights that are explicitly stated in the constitution come together to create a right to privacy. In the world of procedural law, it must be remembered, if the Supreme Court of the United States says it, it is so.

The right to privacy places a limit on many forms of police conduct, from searches to arrest. It is important, however, to understand there is a limit to how far the right goes. It is not absolute. The police are not prohibited from interfering with a citizen's privacy interest, but it must be *reasonable* when they do so.

When it comes to the police conducting searches of people, vehicles, homes, offices and anywhere else a person has a right to privacy, the idea of reasonableness comes down to probable cause. Probable cause means that there is sufficient evidence to make a reasonable person would believe that the person is doing something contrary to the law.

Searches

Police activity that the courts consider a search must be based on probable cause, but remember that the courts define a search differently that the everyday use of the term. There are many exceptions to the probable cause requirement that, while the average person may consider the police conduct a search, it is not considered so by the courts. Objects in **plain view**, for example, are not subject to the probable cause standard, nor are things located in **open fields**. When the probable cause standard does apply because the courts consider a particular police action a search, the police are not allowed to determine if there is in fact probable cause. That job goes to the courts.

Search warrants

An officer desiring to conduct a search needs probable cause for the search to be lawful. Because society expects police officers to find evidence and arrest criminals, they may be overzealous in determining whether the do or do not have probable cause. As a general rule, the evidence establishing probable cause must be submitted to an **impartial magistrate**, and if the magistrate agrees that probable cause exists, then he or she will issue a **search warrant**.

Probable Cause

For a warrant to be issued, the magistrate must determine that probable cause exists. This has to be in the form of a sworn statement called an **affidavit**. When determining probable cause for a search, the reasonableness test used by the courts considers the experience and training of police officers. That is, the test is not merely what a *reasonable person* would believe, but what a reasonable *police officer* would believe in light of the evidence as well as the officer's training and experience. Note that the standard for establishing probable cause is *more likely than not*. This is a far lesser standard that the proof beyond a reasonable doubt standard required for a conviction in criminal court.

The Particularity Requirement

Another requirement for a search warrant to be valid is that it must particularly describe the person or thing to be seized. There are many supreme court cases that establish what this means in particular circumstances. As a general rule regarding search warrants, it means that the place to be searched is sufficiently described that it cannot be confused with some other place.

Obtaining and Executing a Search Warrant

The warrant application process varies in exact detail from jurisdiction to jurisdiction. Often, the Supreme Court of the state in which the warrant is sought provides the details in a legal document known as the **Rules of Criminal Procedure**. The basic rules, however, are dictated by the Supreme Court as interpretations of the Fourth Amendment. All of the officer's evidence must be contained in an affidavit. The rules also dictated how a warrant must be executed. As a general rule, the warrant must be served during daylight hours, and officers must identify themselves as officers and request entry into the place to be searched. This identification requirement is known as ***knock and announce***.

No-knock Warrants

The general rule that officers must "knock and announce" when serving a warrant is not absolute, but special permission from a judge must be obtained before it can be lawfully circumnavigated. A **no-knock warrant** can be issued have a legitimate fear that announcing their presence would endanger lives or give criminals time to destroy evidence. Such a warrant authorizes law enforcement to break down doors without warning and to enter a structure. These types of warrants are controversial. Civil liberty advocates say that such warrants violate the spirit of the Fourth Amendment. Police defend such warrants on the grounds that they save lives and very frequently result in the seizure of contraband.

Searches Without Warrants

There are several exceptions to the general requirement that officers must obtain search warrant for a search to be legal. The Supreme Court has determined that **exigent circumstances** justify an exception to the rule. Exigency is another word for emergency. Thus an exigent circumstances search is an entry into a place that would otherwise require an warrant but for the emergency situation.

Another common warrantless search is a **consent search**. Most of the rights guaranteed by the constitution can be waived by the person that has the right. If a person gives the police permission to search, so long as the permission is given voluntarily, then there is no violation of the person's Fourth Amendment rights. A shocking amount of criminal convictions come as a result of consent searches. Many criminals do not do what is in their legal best interest. According to the Supreme Court of the United States, the police are not obligated to inform citizens that they have the right to refuse consent. Some state courts (e.g. Arkansas), however, have interpreted state constitutions to give this right.

Another exception to the general requirement that police have a warrant to conduct a search is known as a **hot pursuit search**. If an officer chases an offender into a private place, there is no legal requirement that the officer break off the pursuit. If contraband is discovered in such a pursuit, it can be seized and will be admissible in court.

Most of the exceptions to the warrant requirement above do not, for one reason or another, require probable cause. An **automobile search** is an interesting hybrid because it does require probable cause to obtain a warrant, even though the officer is not obligated to actually obtain the warrant. The court allows this compromise because of the inherent mobility of vehicles. The criminal suspect could simply drive away of the officer were required to leave the scene and go obtain a warrant. Merely citing the driver for a traffic violation, however, is not sufficient to establish probable cause for a lawful search.

To preserve evidence and to protect officers from hidden weapons, officers are allowed to search a person after they have been arrested. Such a search is known as a *search incident to arrest*. As an extension of this idea, the officer may search the area immediately surrounding the arrested person. That is, the area immediately under the arrestee's control. The Court has ruled the fact that the suspect is in handcuffs and could not reach for a weapon is immaterial.

Arrests

The Supreme Court has determined that an arrest is a seizure of the person for legal purposes. Accordingly, the Fourth Amendment prohibition against unreasonable searches and seizures comes into play. A person is generally considered to have been arrested when they are taken into custody with the purpose of being charged with a crime.

Most arrests are made without **arrest warrants**, despite the constitution's general requirement that officers have one. Under all circumstances, an officer must have probable cause to make an arrest. When it comes to arrests, probable cause means that the officer has reasonable grounds to believe that the person has committed or is about to commit a crime. When a warrant is sought, the supporting evidence must be included in an affidavit, just as with a search warrant.

The old common law rule was that an officer could make an arrest, without a warrant, if he believed he had evidence amounting probable cause that the person had committed a felony. In the case of a misdemeanor, the crime had to be committed in the officer's presence. These same basic common law rules are still followed in many jurisdictions today. Many jurisdictions, however, have created special rules where misdemeanors that the officer did not witness directly (such as with many domestic battery statutes) can result in lawful arrests without a warrant. Such rules are usually created by state legislatures as a matter of statute.

Arrest Warrants

As previously described, an arrest warrant is a document issued by a court ordering any law enforcement officer to take a particular individual into custody. While there are many exceptions, there are times when a warrant is required to make a lawful arrest. To enter a person's home to make an arrest, the police must have an arrest warrant. (To enter the home of someone other than the person to be arrested to make an arrest, the police must have a search warrant). Of course, the exigent circumstances exception can be applied to arrest warrants just as it can with search warrants.

Domestic Violence Arrests

Social scientific research as resulted in at least some evidence that arresting the **primary aggressor** in domestic violence cases prevents further battering. This research spawned legislation in many states that require police to identify and arrest the primary aggressor in domestic violence situations. While these offenses are generally classified as misdemeanors, these special legislative enactments command law enforcement to take the primary aggressor into custody despite not having a warrant or having seen the crime take place. Despite such laws being in place in many jurisdictions since the 1970s, many police departments do a poor job in dealing with domestic violence cases.

Terry Stops

Making an arrest is a substantial interference with a citizen's constitutionally protected freedom. As such, it requires probable cause. The courts have ruled that there are sorts of intrusions that are less than an arrest, and thus require a lesser standard of evidence. Because the Supreme Court described this sort of situation in a 1968 case styled ***Terry v. Ohio***, these types of "stops" are often referred to as **Terry stops**. In *Terry*, the court said that the police have the right to stop individuals for a short period of time when their behavior seems suspicious, ask them questions, and pat them down for weapons. This type of stop is also known as a **stop and frisk**. The evidentiary standard set forth in *Terry* was less than probable cause, but more than a **mere hunch**. The court called this standard **reasonable suspicion**. Unlike courtroom testimony, reasonable suspicion can be based on hearsay.

The Exclusionary Rule

As previously discussed, the Supreme Court of the United States can tell law enforcement officers how to treat people as long as they have a constitutional reason for doing so. What happens if the cops do not listen to the Court and violate somebody's rights? There are several **remedies**, but the most important one to the criminal justice system is the *exclusionary rule*. The exclusionary rule is very simple. It states that illegally obtained evidence cannot be admitted into a criminal court. Here, *illegally obtained* means obtained in violation of the defendant's constitutional rights. In practice, the defendant's attorney must file a motion to suppress the evidence before trial. The judge will then review the evidence, and if the judge determines that it was obtained in violation of the defendant's rights, it will be suppressed, and the jury will never see the evidence. Its existence cannot even be mentioned at trial.

The exclusionary rule was established by the U.S. Supreme Court in 1914 in the case of ***Weeks v. U.S***. At that time, the rule only applied to Federal agents. States were on their own to decide whether to allow illegally obtained evidence into state courts. It was not until 1961 in *Mapp v. Ohio* that the Court decided that the exclusionary rule was fundamental to a fair trial and was thus applicable to the state via the Fourteenth Amendment's due process clause. The liberal Warren Court decided *Mapp*. Since the time of the warren court, the Supreme Court has become more and more conservative. Conservative justices, while not willing to overrule the basic premise of the exclusionary rule, have eroded it by creating various exceptions. For example, in the 1984 case of ***U.S. v. Leon***, the court created a *good faith exception*. The good faith exception states that if the police are acting on a warrant they believe to be valid and a court later determines that the warrant is invalid, the evidence can still be used in court.

The Fifth Amendment

The common expression "to plead the fifth" refers to the Fifth Amendment to the United States Constitution. The Fifth Amendment gives criminal defendants the right to remain silent, and thus is a right against self-incrimination. The Fifth Amendment has an enormous impact on the practice of police interrogations.

In the days before the civil rights revolution, the police would use any means necessary to gain a confession. Torture, both physical and psychological, was shockingly common. Threats were often used.

The problem with confessions made under such duress is that innocent persons may well confess to crimes simply to make the pain stop. The first major case prohibiting this sort of conduct was ***Brown v. Mississippi*** (1936).

The right against self-incrimination is not as broad as it may first seem. It applies only to confessions. That is, communications that are considered "testimonial" in court. The protection does not extend to physical evidence, so a suspect can be compelled to give fingerprints, DNA samples, blood tests, blood alcohol tests, and so forth. Just as with most constitutional rights, a person can knowingly and voluntarily waive the right to remain silent. If it were not for such waivers, the art of interrogation would hold little value for police.

Confessions and Counsel

The Court has linked the Fifth Amendment right against self-incrimination to the right to counsel. In the case of ***Escobedo v. Illinois*** (1964), the Court ruled that when police questioning moves from merely investigatory to accusatory in nature, the right to counsel becomes active. In other words, once a witness develops into a suspect, then the right to comes into play.

Miranda Warnings

Ultimately, the court was not satisfied with the scope of the protections set forth in *Escobedo*. Two years later, the court established specific interrogation procedures to ensure the Fifth Amendment rights of criminal defendants in *Miranda v. Arizona* (1966). In this landmark case, a man named Miranda confessed to kidnapping and rape. Police obtained the confession without a lawyer being present and without advising Miranda that he had the right to remain silent. The Court held that Miranda was entitled to such a warning, and thus his confession was inadmissible.

The decision in Miranda reached far beyond Miranda's case. It obliged every police officer in America to advise suspects if their rights before asking them questions while in custody. In addition to being advised of the right to remain silent, suspects must be advised that anything that they do say can be used against them in court, that they have the right to an attorney, and that if they cannot afford an attorney they will be provided one by the state. Of course, the suspect may knowingly and voluntarily waive any or all of these rights. The right to remain silent can be invoked at any time. In other words, even if suspects waive their right to remain silent, they can stop the questioning at any time, and must be provided with a lawyer if they so request.

Many police officers and conservative commentators at the time regarded *Miranda* as a legal technicality created by the courts to handcuff the police. On several occasions, increasingly conservative courts have refused to overrule *Miranda*, but they have weakened it by creating several exceptions to it. For example, in ***New York v. Quarles*** (1984), the Court created a **public safety exception**. The public safety exception allows officers to ask questions without giving the *Miranda* warnings if there is some exigency involving the public safety is involved. In ***Nix v. Williams*** (1984), the court created the **inevitable discover exception**. This controversial exception means that if the police would have inevitably discovered the evidence without benefit of the improper questioning, then the evidence will be admissible.

There are many situations in which the person may not necessarily feel free to leave, but they are not in "custody" for *Miranda* purposes. For example, Miranda does not come into play when the police stop a person to (briefly) talk to them on the street, or during traffic stops. Other circumstances do not invoke *Miranda* because there is no questioning of the suspect involved. For example, if a person confesses to an officer without the officer asking any questions, then *Miranda* does not apply.

Police Use of Force

Police officers have the lawful authority to use force, but only if that force is reasonably necessary to accomplish a legitimate criminal justice purpose. Obviously, taking a person into custody by making an arrest, or preventing a suspect from fleeing are examples of legitimate criminal justice purposes. Most questions about the legitimacy of police use of force revolve around the reasonableness of it. If too much force is used, then the use of force will not be lawful. The problem is that defining how much force is necessary in a given situation is a highly subjective process. When the police use more force than someone regards as reasonable in a given situation, it is often referred to as **police brutality**.

Civil Liability and Criminal Prosecution

When the police go beyond reasonable, legitimate use of force, they risk law suits and criminal charges. Under the laws of most states, individual police officers can be sued for torts, such as wrongful death and false imprisonment. There are also federal remedies in place, such as **1983 suits**.

Deadly Force

As one would expect, police officers have the legal right to use deadly force (most often a shooting) when they reasonably believe that they are in imminent danger of serious bodily harm or death. That right extends to the protection of others. Until the court's decision in *Tennessee v. Garner* (1985), many jurisdictions subscribed to the idea of the **fleeing felon rule**. The *fleeing felon rule* was the common law doctrine that allowed an officer to use deadly force to apprehend a felon that was seeking to escape custody or a lawful arrest. In *Tennessee v. Garner*, the court struck down a Tennessee statute stating "if, after notice of the intention to arrest the defendant, he either flee or forcibly resist, the officer may use all the necessary means to effect the arrest." This, in effect, declared the fleeing felon rule unconstitutional. With the abolishment of the fleeing felon rule, the standard become one of dangerousness.

Law Enforcement Jobs Outlook

According to the Bureau of Labor Statistics (2013), the median income for police officers and detectives in 2010 (the most recent statistics available) was $55,010 per year (or $26.45 per hour). There were 794,300 such jobs in the United States, and the expected growth rate over the next decade is projected to be around 7%. Of course, this does not reflect the fact that local political and economic conditions are a major factor in any particular agency's decision to hire new officers. The prediction is that local agencies will do most of the new hiring, and that federal jobs will remain very competitive. According to the BJS, average starting salaries for entry-level local police officers in 2007 ranged from $26,600 per year in the smallest jurisdictions to $49,500 in the largest. Overall, the average starting salary earned by entry-level officers was about $40,500. More than 90% of local police departments serving 25,000 or more residents were using in-field computers during 2007. This suggests that those looking to careers in law enforcement should develop computer skills.

Key Terms

1983 Suit, Affidavit, Arrest Warrant, Automobile Search, *Brown v. Mississippi* **(1936), Consent Search,** *Escobedo v. Illinois* **(1964), Exigent Circumstances Exception, Fleeing Felon Rule, Hot Pursuit Search, Inevitable Discovery Exception, Knock and Announce, Mere Hunch,** *New York v. Quarles* **(1984),** *Nix v. Williams* **(1984), No-knock Warrant, Open Fields Doctrine, Particularity Requirement, Plain View Doctrine, Police Brutality, Primary Aggressor, Public Safety Exception, Reasonable Person Test, Reasonable Suspicion, Remedy, Right to Remain Silent, Rules of Criminal Procedure, Sixth Amendment, Stop and Frisk,** *Tennessee v. Garner* **(1985),** *Terry* **Stop,** *U.S. v. Leon* **(1984),** *Weeks v. U.S.* **(1914)**

Chapter 5: Courts and Sentencing

After the police arrest a person and the investigation is concluded, the case file is turned over to the prosecutor. It is at this stage that the courtroom workgroup takes over from the police. This section will examine the role of the prosecution, the role of the defense, and the role of the court in moving a criminal case forward through the criminal justice system.

Section 5.1: State and Federal Courts

Learning Objectives

After completing this section, you should be able to:

5.1(a)   Describe the structure of the federal court system.
5.1(b)   Compare and contrast the roles of the state and federal court systems.
5.1(c)   Describe the various names and functions of the lower courts.
5.1(d)   Compare and contrast courts of general jurisdiction with courts of appellate jurisdiction.
5.1(e)   Compare and contrast the role of juvenile court judges with trial judges in the adult criminal justice system.
5.1(f)   Discuss the important problems faced by the courts today referencing proposed solutions to those problems.

Introduction

The U.S. court system is very complex due to dual federalism. Each level of government—state, local, and federal—has its own courts. Perhaps the easiest criminal court system to understand is the federal system. When an act violates a federal criminal law, the suspect is tried in federal court. When a suspect violates a state law, it can be tried at the local or state level, depending on the state.

This disparity occurs because each state has its own court system. No two of the fifty are exactly alike. In addition, the federal government operates courts within each of the fifty states. The vast majority of criminal cases are tried in state courts. Most state court systems and the federal court system can be described as hierarchical or "pyramid shaped."

Lower Courts

At the bottom of the court hierarchy are the **lower courts**. The majority of cases heard by these courts are traffic violations and misdemeanor cases. The names vary widely, depending on the state. Municipal courts, police courts, and traffic courts are common examples. There are also many specialized courts at this level. Juvenile courts, for example, often exist at this level.

These courts tend to hear relatively minor matters. Many can, however, sentence violators to jail and impose large fines. Some of these courts also deal with preliminary matters in criminal cases, such as conducting arraignments and preliminary hearings. These felony cases are subsequently transferred to a higher court for trial. Many people—especially those appearing in them—are critical of the "assembly line" justice offered by many municipal courts.

Courts of General Jurisdiction

While the lower courts can only hear nonserious matters, this level of the court system can hear felony cases. **Courts of general jurisdiction** are the trial courts of record of the state court systems. Generally, these courts operate more formally and professionally than the lower courts. There are fewer of them. The name varies depending on the state; in some states, they are called district courts, and in others, they are called circuit courts. This can be very confusing in states that are the reverse of the federal system (where district courts are trial courts and circuit courts are appellate courts). Only a small fraction of cases filed by prosecutors ever go to full trial in these courts. The vast majority end in a plea bargain.

Courts of Appellate Jurisdiction

When a party is dissatisfied with the results of a trial, then they can appeal to a higher court. Appellate courts mostly hear appeals cases, and are higher up in the court hierarchy. The number of levels of appeals courts depends largely on the population of the state. In states with relatively small populations, the losing party at trial can appeal directly to the state's highest court, the state supreme court. In larger states, there is usually an intermediate appeals court that lightens the workload of the state supreme court.

The supreme courts usually have a broad discretion in deciding whether to hear a case or not. The judges are free in many circumstances to decide what cases are important, and to only hear those.

The Federal Court System

Federal courts are organized along very similar lines to state courts, although the more general subject matter jurisdiction of federal courts makes them more streamlined that many state systems.

U.S. District Courts

In the hierarchy of courts, the trial courts of general jurisdiction are always near the bottom. At the federal level, these workhorses of the court system are the 94 U.S. District Courts. Every state in the United States has at least one district court, and some states have several. According to an annual report entitled *Judicial Business of the U.S. Courts* (2014), "filings for criminal defendants (including defendants transferred from other districts) fell 3 percent to 91,266 in 2013. This was the lowest total since 2008." Drug offenses counted for the largest percentage of these filings at around 32% of all criminal cases. Shifts in enforcement strategies have seen a dramatic decline in federal prosecutions for marijuana-related offenses, with an 8% drop in 2013 over the previous year. Immigration, fraud, and firearms related crime made up the bulk of remaining cases.

U.S. Courts of Appeals

Above the federal district courts in the federal court hierarchy are the U.S. Courts of Appeal. They serve mostly to hear appeals from the district courts. Appeals judges do not sit alone when deciding cases, but rather sit in panels of three judges. Rare and important cases are sometimes heard *en banc*, meaning all of the judges in that circuit hear the case together.

These courts lack the discretion of which cases they hear that the Supreme Court enjoys. The docket of the appeals courts is dictated by the number and types of appeals that are filed. Filings in the 12 regional courts of appeals fell 2 percent to 56,475. Decreases occurred in filings of criminal appeals, appeals of administrative agency decisions, and civil appeals. Growth was reported for prisoner petitions, bankruptcy appeals, and original proceedings (Administrative Office of the U.S. Courts, 2014).

The U.S. Supreme Court (USSC)

The U.S. Supreme Court crowns the hierarchy of United States Courts. It hears appeals that come out of both federal and state courts. Considering there are only nine justices, the workload of the Supreme Court is very heavy. The Supreme Court is different than lower level courts in that they exercise **certiorari power**. This means that the justices get to decide which cases to review and which to pass over. The cases that they do select tend to have very broad national implications. Because the Supreme Court functions mostly as a court of appeals, most of the cases they decide result in a lower court's decision either being **affirmed** or **reversed**.

Problems with the Courts

One of the biggest problems facing the courts today is the high volume of cases. For example, in 2013, combined filings for civil cases and criminal defendants in the U.S. district courts totaled 363,914. According to the Court Statistics Project, over 10.6 million cases were processed in state trial courts in 2009 (the last year for which data is available).

The tough drug sanctions of the recent past caused a steadily increasing caseload for the courts. A majority of state courts are perpetually behind on hearing cases. Accordingly, there has been an increasing interest on both the state and federal level with how to reduce caseloads and speed up the flow of cases.

Reducing Caseloads

Perhaps the most popular effort to reduce caseloads has been the advent of *drug courts*. A big difference between drug courts and regular courts is that drug courts tend to sentence nonviolent, first-time offenders to drug treatment rather than probation or prison. The main purposes of drug courts are to reduce recidivism and reduce the caseload of the regular courts. The empirical research suggests that drug courts are more effective at reducing recidivism than traditional probation or prison.

Speeding Up Court Processing

When there are too many cases being processed by the courts, the speed at which cases can be processes slows down, sometimes dramatically. This is especially problematic in criminal courts where defendants have a constitutional guarantee of a speedy trial. For this and other reasons, the public is dissatisfied when case resolution becomes a long, drawn-out process.

At the federal level, there has been legislation to force the courts to run faster. **The Speedy Trail Act of 1974** sets time standards for two different stages in the federal progression. The law stipulates that the prosecutor has a maximum of thirty days from the time of arrest to arraign a suspect, and an additional seventy days from the indictment to the trial. Every state has followed the federal example by enacting some form of speedy trial law.

The Role of Judges

The many responsibilities of the trial court judge extend throughout the entire criminal court process. From the time of an arrest, judges make critical decisions that have a deep impact on the cases and lives of those accused of crimes. Because they must evaluate probable cause and issue search and arrest warrants, judges are often involved in criminal cases before an arrest takes place. Once the offender is arrested, the judge must decide if bail is to be granted, the amount of bail, rule on pretrial motions made by both the prosecution and the defense, hear pleas, referee trials, and pass sentences. At all stages of the process, the judge must perform a balancing act, protecting the rights of the accused while also protecting the best interest of the public. Appeals court judges have different responsibilities than trial judges. While trial judges are mostly referees in the adversarial battle between prosecution and defense, appeals court judges serve as legal scholars by researching, clarifying, and writing opinions on legal issues.

Federal Judges

Federal judges tend to be the cream of the crop. They tend to come from families with a long history of public service and attend the finest law schools in the world. Some critics argue that those families are also wealthy, and that federal judges are selected from the social and cultural elite and that the process is unfair.

State Judges

State level judges tend to be drawn heavily from whichever political party dominates that particular state. There are a variety of ways that judges are selected, depending on state law. Some states have partisan elections, meaning that candidates for judgeships run under the banner of a particular political party. In other states, judges are elected, but they run as nonpartisan candidates, meaning that they state no allegiance to a particular political party. Some states use an appointment system, where the governor of the state appoints judges. Still other states select judges by legislative appointment. Some states, such as Missouri, use a merit system.

Judicial Decision Making

The very nature of being a judge requires making important decisions. Judges make decisions that have an enormous impact on the lives of defendants. Trial court judges are often called upon to make decisions in an instant, while appeals court judges have more time to ponder weighty issues and seek input from colleagues and staff.

Because of the doctrine of *stare decisis*, the decisions of judges are tempered by the existing legal landscape. That is, most judges follow precedent when it is available, and try to use the legal logic of past cases to guide them when novel legal questions arise. Political values often come into play, although these are not as readily recognized as is legal tradition.

Judicial Misconduct

Judges have an awesome amount of power, and this power sometimes corrupts. Judges, like other criminal justice professionals, sometimes act in unethical and illegal ways. These inappropriate activities undermine the public confidence in the judiciary and create injustice. Each state has some sort of mechanism in place to deal with unethical conduct by judges. At the federal level, judges can only be removed by impeachment by the Senate.

Judicial Independence

The founding fathers decided early on that the courts should be independent of the other branches of government. There are several reasons for this separation of powers. Perhaps the most important reason for judicial independence is that it allows judges to preside over cases in a just and impartial way. Another important reason is that the courts serve as a check on the power of the executive and legislative branches.

It is a mistake, however, to view the judiciary as completely independent. The other branches of government have the ability to influence the judiciary. The executive often has the power of appointment over judges. The legislative branch has the power of the purse, controlling the budget of the courts. These powers, while significant, are limited. Federal judges, for example, are appointed for life tenure. That means that once appointed by the executive, they cannot be fired. The founding fathers formed government in this way because they understood that a judge fearful of losing his job could not be a neutral and detached magistrate that is willing to rule against the legislative or the executive.

Juveniles and the Courts

Just as with the adult criminal justice system, the courts powerfully influence the juvenile justice system. This is true at both the juvenile court level, and at the appellate level.

Juvenile Courts

Perhaps the most important member of the juvenile justice system is the juvenile court judge. Juvenile judges have the role of a traditional judge, but this role is greatly expanded when a judge presides over a juvenile court. In many jurisdictions, the juvenile judge oversees not only the operations of the juvenile court, but juvenile probation departments as well. In many small jurisdictions, juvenile court judges are responsible for the fiscal management of the courts as well as probation departments.

The beliefs, attitudes, and behaviors of juvenile judges can have an incredible impact on other criminal justice agencies in particular, and the entire community in general. For example, judges that do a poor job of dealing with juvenile delinquency in the schools runs the risk of creating a disruptive and lawless learning environment. At the other end of the spectrum, judges that are overly punitive in their decisions run the risk of violating the doctrine of *parens patriae*.

Much of what juvenile court judges do can be described as a balancing act. Juvenile judges must ensure that all processes and decisionmaking are carried out in a fair and unbiased manner. They must make sure that all decisions balance the best interests of the juvenile with the best interests of the victim and community. In addition, they must ensure that the constitutional rights of all parties are upheld. While the juvenile justice system is substantially different than the adult system, constitutional guarantees of due process must be upheld in juvenile proceedings. In practice, this requirement creates an often-uncomfortable conflict of adversarial process versus the best interest of the child.

The Supreme Court & Juveniles

Historically, juvenile proceedings rarely made it to the U.S. Supreme Court. Starting with the Warren court in the 1960s, however, the Supreme Court handed down several cases that dramatically altered the structure and function of the juvenile justice system.

Landmark Court Decisions in Juvenile Justice	
Kent v. United States (1966)	Held that juveniles must be afforded due process rights in court proceedings.
In re Gault (1967)	Held that juveniles accused of crimes must be afforded many of the same due process rights as adults.
Breed v. Jones (1975)	Held that finding a child delinquent in a juvenile court then trying the child in adult court amounts to double jeopardy.
Schall v. Martin (1984)	Held that the preventive detention of a juvenile does not necessarily violate due process.
Doe v. Renfrow (1981)	Upheld a lower court decision that a search of schoolchildren for narcotics by a drug dog is not rights violation.
New Jersey v. TLO (1985)	Set the evidentiary standard for searches of students by school officials at reasonable suspicion.
Qutb v. Strauss (1993)	Held that curfew laws were constitutional because they are designed to protect the community.

Key Terms

Affirmed, Assembly Line Justice, Certiorari Power, Courts of General Jurisdiction, *Doe v. Renfrow* (1981), Judicial Independence, Judicial Misconduct, *Kent v. United States* (1966), Lower Courts, Municipal Courts, *New Jersey v. TLO* (1985), Police Courts, *Qutb v. Strauss* (1993), Reversed, Speedy Trial Act of 1974, Traffic Courts, U.S. Courts of Appeal, U.S. District Courts

Section 5.2: The Prosecution and Defense

Learning Objectives

After completing this section, you should be able to:

5.2(a)   Describe the role of the defense attorney in a criminal trial.
5.2(b)   Trace the history of indigent defense in the United States.
5.2(c)   Describe the role of the prosecutor in a criminal trial in the United States.
5.2(d)   Describe important areas in the criminal justice process where prosecutors have nearly unlimited discretion.
5.2(e)   Trace the philosophical underpinnings of the juvenile justice system in the United States.

Introduction

Recall that the United States has an *adversarial* legal system. This means that all criminal matters decided by the courts are a contest between a lawyer for the state and (in most cases) a lawyer for the defense. These "adversaries" are ethically required to do their utmost to prevail in court.

Prosecutors

Prosecutors at the federal level prosecute different types of crimes than their state court counterparts. Regardless of the level of government, it is the prosecutor's job to present the government's case against criminal defendants. The purpose of this is to demonstrate guilt to the finder of fact. This often involves working with law enforcement personnel to ensure that evidence is in order prior to launching criminal proceedings. It is also among the duties of the prosecutor to see that justice is done; this can mean sharing evidence that tends to prove the defendant's guilt.

U.S. Attorneys

In federal courts, prosecutors are known as **United States Attorneys**. All 94 federal court districts in the United States have a U.S. Attorney. They are appointed by the President, and function mainly as administrators. Assistant U.S. Attorneys usually conduct actual prosecutions. The Attorney General of the United States, who also heads up the United States Department of Justice, supervises U.S. Attorneys. The almost 2,000 assistant federal prosecutors investigate violations of federal laws, focusing on matters beyond the scope of local law enforcement operations, such as public corruption, large scale drug trafficking, and white collar crime.

District Attorneys

At the state and local level of government, prosecutors are usually called **District Attorneys (D.A.)**. Some jurisdictions, such as Illinois, call these government lawyers State's Attorneys. District Attorneys have a large amount of discretion. Official action for prosecutorial misconduct is rare, and different jurisdictions deal with it in different ways.

City Attorneys

Some jurisdictions allow for the prosecution of violations and some misdemeanors at the local level. These **City Attorneys** prosecute minor offenses that often only result in fines such as traffic offenses, nuisance offenses, and violations involving alcohol. Some jurisdictions allow these attorneys to prosecute misdemeanor cases that can result in jail time.

Independent Counsels

Independent counsels are lawyers that serve as prosecutors in cases where high-level government officials are charged with misconduct. The reason they exist is to prevent the abuse of government power. The U.S. attorney general has the power to appoint an independent counsel when he or she determines that there is sufficient evidence to warrant the investigation of high-ranking government officials, including members of the United States Congress. These independent counsels are not accountable to any government office. This is to prevent undue influence over the investigation. Independent counsels serve in this capacity for as long as is necessary to complete the investigation.

Prosecutorial Discretion

Prosecutors arguably have the most discretion of any actor in the criminal justice system. They make decisions as to who to charge, what to charge them with, when charges should be dropped, and whether or not to plea bargain. Because of this charging power in death penalty states, some prosecutors literally hold the power of life and death. While the discretion of prosecutors is nearly unfettered, it is most commonly used in three main areas: the discretionary decisions to file charges, dismiss charges, and offer plea bargains.

Charging

While police initially inform criminal defendants of the charges against them, it is up to the prosecutor to decide what the exact formal charges will be. First, however, the prosecutor must make the decision to prosecute persons accused by the police, or to not prosecute them. The decision to prosecute is linked to several factors. Perhaps the most important factor is the strength of the evidence against the accused. Obviously, prosecutors do not like to move forward with cases they cannot win. The seriousness of the offense is another important factor. Offenses that are more serious are more likely to be prosecuted. Other factors are resource based. The prosecutor must consider both prosecutorial resources and the size of the court's docket. Community resources are also important. Prosecutors can only seek alternatives to prosecution and prison when those resources are available. The characteristics of the defendant are important as well. The defendant's degree of culpability and criminal history factor into the equation, influencing the prosecutor to prosecute more aggressively and to seek harsher punishments. Cooperation with the police and a willingness to help prosecute others influence the prosecutor to seek lighter sentences.

Dropping Charges

Once charges are filed by a prosecutor, there is still a wide discretion as to how to move the case forward. The prosecutor can decide to go forward to trial with the case. An alternative is to make a plea bargain where the defendant is offered a lighter sentence for a guilty plea. The prosecutor can also enter a

nolle prosequi. A *nolle prosequi* is a formal statement by a prosecutor stating that a case will be dropped. Prosecutors can enter a nolle prosequi (often abbreviated as *nol. pros.*) when the case is deemed trivial, evidence is determined by the court to be inadmissible, there is insufficient evidence, and when it is discovered that false accusations were made.

Plea Bargaining

Prosecutors have a great deal of discretion when negotiating **plea bargains** with the defense. A plea bargain is an agreement in which the prosecutor permits the defendant to plead guilty in exchange for concessions such as reduced charges or lenient sentence recommendations. Both the prosecution and the defense can benefit from plea bargains. For the defense, the obvious benefit is a reduced sentence. For the prosecution, plea bargaining is a matter of conserving resources, both the prosecutor's resources and the courts. If plea bargaining did not occur, the work of the courts would slowly stop.

The Defense

The role of the defense attorney is to champion the defense at every stage adversarial legal process. This role is critical to maintaining fairness in the criminal justice system. Many different tasks are the responsibility of the defense attorney. Defense attorneys protect the rights of the accused in pretrial processes such as police interrogations and lineups. Defense attorneys must work with prosecutors and determine the strength of the cases against their clients. They must represent their clients at bail hearings, suppression hearings, and other pretrial matters. Defense attorneys must devise a defense strategy that can include plea bargaining or going on to trial. When cases do go on to trial, defense attorneys represent their clients in court. When clients are found guilty, defense attorneys represent their clients at sentencing hearings, arguing against the measures proposed by the prosecution. Defense attorneys also represent their clients in appeals when the results of a trial are unfavorable.

Types of Defense

While there are a staggering number of variations when specific details are examined, there are three basic ways that criminal defendants can defend themselves in court: Defendants can hire their own private attorney, they can utilize legal services provided by the government for the poor, or they can represent themselves. Because self-representation is a notoriously bad idea, most criminal defendants choose one of the first two options.

Legal Services for the Indigent

In the criminal justice system, most criminal defendants cannot afford to hire a private lawyer to represent them. Historically, this meant that only the wealthy could have lawyers to represent them in many state courts. In 1963, this situation changed. It was in this year that the Supreme Court handed down the famous ***Gideon v. Wainwright*** decision. In this case, the court held that an **indigent defendant** charged in state courts with a felony offense had a due process right to be represented by counsel. Later, in a 1972 case styled ***Argersinger v. Hamlin***, the court refined this rule by extending the right to court-appointed counsel whenever there was a danger of the defendant being sentenced to prison. This remains the standard today. Those accused of minor offenses that result only in a fine, such as traffic violations, are not entitled to state-funded attorneys.

The term indigent can be misleading. The term *poor* usually define it, but most states do not require that a defendant be without any means at all to qualify for appointed counsel. It is hard to be specific about these requirements because every state makes its own rules. The qualifications are sufficiently broad in scope that more than 80% of criminal defendants accused of a felony use appointed counsel for their defense.

Many advocates believe that free legal defense services are underfunded in the United States because the concept of providing tax-funded legal services to "criminals" is politically unpopular. Many believe that this state of affairs causes unacceptably high case loads, which forces attorneys to recommend actions that are not in the best interest of the client, such as accepting plea bargains.

Retained Counsel

The typical private defense attorney has several years' experience working with criminal cases as a government employee, such as with a prosecutor's office or a public defender's office. Veteran criminal defense attorneys can set very high fees. The amount of fees charged is also related to the complexity of the case and whether the attorney has to appear at trial.

Self-representation

There is an old adage in the legal community that "a lawyer that represents himself in court has a fool for a client." The very nature of our adversarial system makes it very difficult to mount an effective legal defense for one's self. It is nearly impossible, for example, to cross-examine yourself without looking foolish. If this is true for legal professionals, then it is even more so for non-lawyers.

Despite the lack of efficacy, the Supreme Court determined in ***Faretta v. California*** (1975) that the people have a right to self-representation in criminal cases. There are a few restrictions placed on these individuals. The key legal requirement is that the defendants knowingly and voluntarily waive the right to counsel.

Defendant's Rights

Woven into the very fabric of our legal system is the idea that the process should be fair to everyone. Fairness often means that the legal system has to treat every individual the same way, regardless of race, creed, religion, sex, and so forth. This idea that everybody has to be treated by the government in the same, fair way is summed up in the term *procedural due process*. This idea is enshrined in the Bill of Rights, and can be found in both the Fifth and the Fourteenth Amendments.

Some critics argue that these measures serve to protect criminals and should accordingly be done away with. This is not a very carefully considered position. Under our legal system, those accused of crimes are assumed innocent until proven guilty in a court of law. If these rights were not protected for all people, then every citizen, regardless of any wrongdoing, would be subject to searches of their persons, vehicles, and houses. They would be subject to arrest, confinement, and questioning under duress or even torture. Most American's are not willing to accept such blatant abuses of human rights, and so our constitution protects us from them by design. There is just no way to protect the rights of everyday citizens without protecting the rights of criminals along with them until the criminals can be convicted in a court of law.

The Philosophy of the Juvenile System

A central theme of the juvenile justice system is that juveniles should be treated differently than adults. It is assumed that delinquent children, due to a lack of maturity, are less culpable than their adult counterparts are. A critical difference between the juvenile justice system and the adult criminal justice system is that the juvenile justice system is not adversarial in nature, at least philosophically.

Parens Patriae

Early reformers insisted that court proceedings against juveniles were not adversarial, but that the state was proceeding as parens patriae. The Supreme Court has been critical of this idea: "The Latin phrase proved to be a great help to those who sought to rationalize the exclusion of juveniles from the constitutional scheme; but its meaning is murky and its historic credentials are of dubious relevance."

The phrase was taken from chancery practice, where, however, it was used to describe the power of the state to act in *loco parentis* for the purpose of protecting the property interests and the person of the child. But there is no trace of the doctrine in the history of criminal jurisprudence. At common law, children under seven were considered incapable of possessing criminal intent. Beyond that age, they were subjected to arrest, trial, and in theory to punishment like adult offenders. Prior to the splitting of the criminal justice system into an adult court system and a juvenile court system, the state was not considered to have authority to accord children fewer procedural rights than adults.

The right of the state, as *parens patriae*, to deny to the child procedural rights available to adults was justified by the assertion that a child, unlike an adult, has a right "not to liberty but to custody." According to this philosophy, if a child's parents fail in effectively performing their custodial functions—that is, if the child is "delinquent"—the state may intervene. In doing so, the court does not deprive the child of any rights, because, under the parens patriae philosophy, children have no rights. The court merely provides the "custody" to which the child is entitled. On this basis, proceedings involving juveniles were described as "civil" not "criminal" and therefore not subject to the requirements that restrict the state when it seeks to deprive a person of his liberty. While popular for an extended period, this logic did not sit well with the civil rights minded Warren Court.

A Constitutional Shift

Most people agree that the establishment of the juvenile justice system without constitutional safeguards in place was motivated by high ideas and a desire to help children. When put into practice, however, the results were not always satisfactory. The Justices of the Warren Court were critical of the unbridled discretion that juvenile judges had in dealing with children's lives. The intent of the juvenile system was that children would receive careful, compassionate, individualized treatment. At times, the Court argued, these intentions did not translate into fair, efficient, and effective procedures. A review of juvenile court procedures led the Warren Court to conclude that a departure from well-established standards of due process resulted in arbitrary and capricious treatment of juveniles.

It was for these and other reasons that the Supreme Court became very critical of the philosophy not working in practice: "It is claimed that juveniles obtain benefits from the special procedures applicable to them which more than offset the disadvantages of denial of the substance of normal due process. ...the observance of due process standards, intelligently and not ruthlessly administered, will not compel the States to abandon or displace any of the substantive benefits of the juvenile process. But it is important, we think, that the claimed benefits of the juvenile process should be candidly appraised." The result of that appraisal was a shift toward constitutional safeguards in juvenile courts.

Key Terms

Argersinger v. Hamlin (1972), Assistant U.S. Attorney, City Attorney, District Attorney (D.A.), Docket, *Faretta v. California* (1975), Independent Counsel, Indigent Defendant, *Nolle Prosequi*, State's Attorney, United States Attorney

Section 5.3: Pretrial Process

Learning Objectives

After completing this section, you should be able to:

5.3(a)   List and describe the steps typically taken by both the prosecution and defense in the pretrial phase.
5.3(b)   Explain the concept of pretrial release, and the circumstances under which it may be denied.
5.3(c)   Discuss the practice of plea bargaining and why it is a necessary part of the criminal justice process.
5.3(d)   Describe the jury selection process.
5.3(e)   Compare and contrast the workings of a grand jury with a petit (trial) jury.
5.3(f)   List and describe the steps typically taken in processing a case through juvenile court.

Introduction

Television legal dramas have trained the American people to understand that all of the important legal maneuverings in a criminal case takes place in a courtroom in front of a judge and jury. This conception can safely be included among the myths of criminal justice. Consider that over 90% of criminal charges result in a guilty plea and never go to trial. Most of these are the result of a plea bargain agreement hammered out between the prosecution (the state) and the defense. The fact is that many important legal steps are taken prior to trial. These steps make for a functional criminal justice system but are not good drama, so they never get the spotlight on television.

The Right to an Attorney

Counsel, either hired by the defendant or appointed by the court, represents almost every criminal defendant in both state and federal courts. Defendants representing themselves are far more common with misdemeanors. There is a common belief that appointed lawyers do not do as good a job defending their clients as do privately hired attorneys. In a report issued by the Bureau of Justice Statistics (Harlow, 2002), it was found that there was very little difference between how counsel was obtained on the verdict of guilty. However, it was also found that among those receiving a guilty verdict, a higher percentage of defendants with appointed counsel were sentenced to incarceration. The BJS study also found that the rate of entering a guilty plea was higher with appointed counsel. About 75% of inmates with appointed counsel pleaded guilty, while around 66% of those with hired counsel pleaded guilty.

The responsibility for appointing counsel in federal criminal proceedings for those unable to bear the cost of representation has historically rested in the federal judiciary. Before the enactment of the **Criminal Justice Act (CJA)**, however, there was no authority to compensate appointed counsel for their services or litigation expenses, and federal judges depended on the professional obligation of lawyers to provide *pro bono publico* representation to defendants unable to retain counsel (Courts, 2015).

In 1964, the CJA was enacted to establish a comprehensive system for appointing and compensating lawyers to represent defendants financially unable to retain counsel in federal criminal proceedings. The CJA authorized reimbursement of reasonable out-of-pocket expenses and payment of expert and investigative services necessary for an adequate defense. While it provided for some compensation for appointed counsel (CJA panel attorneys), it did so at rates substantially below that which they would receive from their privately-retained clients.

In 1970, the CJA was amended to authorize districts to establish federal defender organizations as counterparts to federal prosecutors in U.S. Attorneys Offices and an institutional resource for providing defense counsel in those districts (or combinations of adjacent districts) where at least 200 persons annually require appointment of counsel.

According to the Administrative Office of the United States Courts, there are now 81 authorized federal defender organizations. They employ more than 3,100 lawyers, investigators, paralegals, and support personnel and serve 91 of the 94 federal judicial districts. There are two types of federal defender organizations: federal public defender organizations and community defender organizations.

Federal defender organizations, together with the more than 10,000 private "panel attorneys" who accept CJA assignments annually, represent the vast majority of individuals who are prosecuted in our nation's federal courts. CJA panel attorneys accept appointments in all CJA cases in the four districts not served by a federal defender organization. In those districts with a defender organization, panel attorneys are typically assigned between 30 percent and 40 percent of the CJA cases, generally those where a conflict of interest or some other factor precludes federal defender representation. Nationwide, federal defenders receive approximately 60 percent of CJA appointments, and the remaining 40 percent are assigned to the CJA panel.

The Decision to Charge

The police may be the gatekeepers of the criminal justice system, but ultimately the decision to prosecute the suspect is up to the prosecutor. Recall that all criminal prosecutions are brought forward by the government, and the prosecutor is the government's lawyer. If the prosecutor decides to move forward with a case, a *charging document* is filed with the court. A charging document formally accuses the suspect with committing a crime. There are two basic types of charging document: An *information* originates with the prosecutor, and an *indictment* originates with a *grand jury*. While these documents differ in many respects, they both contain a formal statement of the charge against the suspect.

Reviewing the Charge

Before criminal cases can move forward to trial, there must be a judicial determination that such a move is justified by the evidence. Often, a lower court judge rather than a judge with jurisdiction in a felony case make this determination. As with many criminal justice tasks, the standard of proof here is *probable cause*.

First Appearance

Several important functions are served by a first appearance. Defendants are informed of the nature of the charges against them. Defendants have their constitutional rights explained to them. If the defendant is indigent (too poor to afford a lawyer), counsel is appointed. The judge also determines if bail will be granted, and if so, how much.

Bail

Conventionally, *bail* entailed money or other valuable property that defendants deposit with the court in order to ensure their appearance in court if they are released prior to trial. If the defendant failed to appear at trial, the money or property was forfeited to the court. Often, courts do not require a cash bail. They release the defendant on a mere personal promise to appear. In other words, they are released on their own recognizance. This is often shortened to **release on recognizance** (ROR). Not all criminal defendants are granted bail. Recall that the constitution prohibits excessive bail, but does not guarantee bail in general. The Supreme Court has determined that when criminal defendants are a flight risk or that they are a danger to the community, then they can be held in jail to await trial. Still others wait on their trial date in jail because they cannot afford bail.

According to the Bureau of Justice Statistics (2007), 62% of felony defendants in State courts in the 75 largest counties were released prior to the disposition of their case. Many critics argue that the current bail system, with an increasing reliance on commercial bail bonding, discriminates against the poor. As one would suspect, the higher the bail, the fewer defendants are released. About 7 in 10 defendants secured release when bail was set at less than $5,000, but this proportion dropped to 1 in 10 when bail was set at $100,000 or more (Cohen & Reaves, 2007).

Perhaps the most important criterion for setting bail is the seriousness of the offense. Those charged with murder are the least likely to receive bail, followed by other serious crimes such as rape, robbery, and burglary. Those charged with less serious offenses and white-collar offenses (e.g., fraud) are the most likely to be released on bail. Another reason that so many defendants do not stay out of jail pending trial is the commission of new offenses. Approximately a third of released defendants were charged with one or more types of pretrial misconduct, and nearly a fourth had a bench warrant issued for failing to appear in court. About a sixth were arrested for a new offense, with more than half of those new arrests were for felonies (Cohen & Reaves, 2007).

Preventive Detention

As a rule, suspects are innocent until proven guilty and are deserving of bail. This is based not on an explicit statement of the right in the Bill of Rights, but was established by the Court in the landmark case of **Coffin v. U.S.** (1895). This U.S. Supreme Court case clearly defined the principle of the presumption of innocence for the first time in U.S. history. Although believed to be inferred from the U.S. Constitution, no direct recognition of this presumption had been previously articulated. The significance of this case is that it places the burden of "proof beyond a reasonable doubt" on the prosecution in criminal proceedings. In reference to setting bail, all defendants are to be presumed innocent prior to adjudication, and thus, not subject to criminal penalties prior to trial.

Many states and the Federal government have statutes that allow judges to deny bail in circumstances where the defendant is a high flight risk. The **Bail Reform Act** (1984) gives federal judges the authority to hold suspects without bail when they are deemed a treat to the public safety. Many civil libertarians argue that this is unconstitutional since it goes against the presumption of innocence.

In **U.S. v. Salerno** (1987), the U.S. Supreme Court upheld the constitutionality of the Bail Reform Act of 1984. This case consisted of an alleged member of an organized crime "mafia family" charged under the **Racketeering and Corrupt Influence Organization (RICO)** statute who was believed to pose a threat to governmental witnesses if released on bond. The challenge was based on the provisions of the Fifth and Eighth Amendments to the U.S. Constitution. The Court held that sufficient evidence was present to detain the subject prior to trial and that a "compelling interest" (i.e., public safety) aside from the risk of nonappearance was presented to warrant the defendant's detention. However, the Court cautioned the judiciary and pretrial services agencies by noting that the United States' system of justice is based on the presumption of innocence and that pretrial release should be "the norm" in the vast majority of criminal cases.

Grand Jury

An arrest by the police is by no means a guarantee that a suspect will go to trial. As previously discussed, a probable cause determination must be made. In some jurisdictions this determination is made by a judge, but in others the decision is made by a panel of citizens. The federal government, along with about half the states, has such a panel of citizens that is known as a *grand jury*. The size of the grand jury varies from jurisdiction to jurisdiction, but they are generally larger than trial (petit) juries, consisting of up to 23 members. In cases where the prosecutor convinces a majority of the grand jury that there is probable cause to support the criminal allegations, the grand jury approves the indictment.

Critics of the grand jury system seem them as antithetical to due process and believe that they should be abolished altogether. Grand jury hearings are held in private, and hearsay evidence is admissible. There is no right of the defendant to have an attorney present at the hearing, and no right to cross-examine witnesses offering testimony against the accused. Grand jury hearings are known as ***ex parte*** proceedings because the defense is not represented.

The grand jury has its origins in antiquity, when citizens needed protection from potentially overzealous prosecution by the Crown. The system began as a protection of civil rights, but now, critics argue, it has become a tool of oppression by the government because the rules so favor the prosecution. Many of the procedural safeguards that are present at criminal trials are not present at grand jury proceedings, such as the exclusionary rule. They argue that because the proceedings are so one sided, they are nothing more than a rubber stamp for the prosecutor.

Preliminary Hearing

In jurisdictions where grand juries are not used, the grand jury proceedings are replaced by a preliminary hearing. In most jurisdictions, attorneys from both sides are present, and a judge presides. For this reason, preliminary hearings are considered an adversarial process. If, after hearing evidence from both sides, the judge determines that probable cause does exist, then he or she sends the case forward to trial.

Arraignment

If a case moves past the probable cause determination process, it will move forward to a trial court that has jurisdiction over the offense charged. At an arraignment, the judge informs the defendant of the charges alleged by the prosecution and asks for a plea from the defendant. The most common pleas available to criminal defendants are **guilty**, **not guilty**, and **nolo contendere**. The nolo contendere plea, meaning "no contest", has the same effect in a criminal trial as a guilty plea, but there is no admission of guilt that can be used against the defendant later in a civil trial. If the defendant pleads not guilty, then the judge sets a trial date.

Pretrial Motions

Before the actual trial begins, both the prosecution and the defense can make several motions. One of the most common pretrial motions is a motion for **discovery**. Discovery is where the prosecution must make available all of the evidence it has to the defendant. The prosecutor is legally and ethically obligated to turn over any **exculpatory** evidence. In other words, if the prosecution has any evidence that tends to prove the defendant's innocence, then it must be turned over to the defense. Also common are **motions to suppress**. A motion to suppress is a request by the defense to disallow illegally obtained evidence from being admitted at trial. If the defense prevails in this motion, the jury will never see the evidence. In other words, a motion to suppress is an attempt by the defense to invoke the exclusionary rule.

Juvenile Process

When a juvenile breaks a criminal law, the process that is followed by the legal system is quite different from the adult criminal justice system's process. The idea that juvenile offenders are different from adults is so fundamental to the American philosophy of justice that separate courts have been established in every state to deal with juvenile issues. A key difference between the juvenile process and the adult process is the enormous amount of discretion that each set of actors—police, courts, and corrections—has in a juvenile case. While the precise process of dealing with juvenile cases varies from jurisdiction to jurisdiction, there are many common rules that must be followed because of constitutional rights that have been defined by the Supreme Court of the United States.

Once law enforcement has decided to turn a case over to the courts (rather than proceeding with an informal diversion), a prosecutor or juvenile intake officer (often a juvenile probation officer) is assigned to the case. The intake officer may choose to dismiss the case, handle the case informally, or file a **petition**. The petition is a formal document alleging wrongdoing by the juvenile, similar to a charging document (information or indictment) in adult criminal court. Depending on the rules of the particular jurisdiction, some juveniles must appear before a judge even though no formal proceedings are begun. These informal appearances before the bench are calculated to help the juvenile understand the seriousness of delinquency.

If the prosecutor decides to begin formal charges, a petition is filed with the court. An arraignment is held, and the juvenile is informed of the charges. Many states have rules that allow older juveniles accused of serious crimes to be sent to adult court. The most common of these waivers to adult court are for violent offenses.

Once formal proceedings have begun, there are three basic options. Like adults, juveniles can often enter into a plea agreement with the state. Such plea agreements usually result in the juvenile being placed on probation and being required to adhere to many rules and conditions. Counseling, curfews, and maintaining certain academic standards are common requirements.

Many juvenile cases are handled through a process of **judicial diversion**. When a juvenile judge diverts a case, some informal sanction or treatment option is usually ordered. Counseling, community service, and victim restitution are often ordered. If the juvenile does not comply with the judge's orders, formal charges can be reinstated.

The final option is for the judge to hold an **adjudicatory hearing**. This is the juvenile justice system's equivalent of a criminal trial. In most states, the hearing will be conducted before a juvenile judge, but there is generally no jury in a juvenile case. At the conclusion of the hearing, the judge will decide whether the allegations are true. If so, the juvenile will be **adjudicated delinquent**. This result is commonly referred to as **sustaining the petition**.

In many cases, the adjudicatory hearing is **bifurcated**. This means that there is a separate **disposition hearing**, which is the juvenile court's equivalent of a sentencing hearing in adult court. Prior to the disposition hearing, a juvenile parole officer will thoroughly assess the juvenile, often with the assistance of mental health professionals. The judge designs a **disposition** in the case based (at least theoretically) on what is in the best interest of the child. Counseling, probation, confinement in a secure detention facility, and victim restitution are common in juvenile dispositions. Juveniles can also be ordered to reappear in court periodically for **post-disposition hearings**. These hearings are designed to update the judge on the juvenile's progress toward reform.

Key Terms

Adjudicated Delinquent, Adjudicatory Hearing, Bail Reform Act (1984), Bifurcated Hearing, *Coffin v. U.S.* (1895), Community Defender Organization, Criminal Justice Act (CJA), Discovery, Disposition, Disposition Hearing, Ex Parte, Exculpatory Evidence, Federal Public Defender Organization, Guilty Plea, Judicial Diversion, Motion to Suppress, Nolo Contendere Plea, Not Guilty Plea, Petition, Post-disposition Hearing, Pretrial Motions, *Pro Bono Publico*, Racketeering and Corrupt Influence Organization (RICO), Release on Recognizance (ROR), Sustaining the Petition, *U.S. v. Salerno* (1987)

Learning Objectives

After completing this section, you should be able to:

5.4(a)   Describe the several stages of a criminal trial.
5.4(b)   Explain the hearsay rule, and describe some exceptions to it.
5.4(c)   Describe how attorneys are provide to indigent defendants in federal courts.
5.4(d)   Explain the role of evidence in a criminal trial referencing the major types.
5.4(e)   Explain the extra procedural requirements for jury decisions in capital cases.

Introduction

The Sixth Amendment has an enormous impact on the criminal trial process. Included among the guarantees are the right to a speedy trial, the right to a public trial, the right to a trial by jury, the right to notice of accusations, the right to confront witnesses against the defense, and the assistance of counsel. These rights are so fundamental to due process that the Supreme Court has applied them to the states via the Fourteenth Amendment's due process clause.

Jury Trials versus Bench Trials

As with most constitutional rights, the defendant can waive the right to a jury trial and opt to have a *bench trial*. A bench trial is a type of trial in which the judge serves as the finder of fact and determines the innocence or guilt of the defendant. Such a trial can be advantageous to the defense when the circumstances of the case are likely to cause hostility in a jury such that emotional reactions are likely. The defendant must make this decision; the state must offer a jury trial to defendants whenever a jail term is possible. This means that there is no right to a jury trial for violations such as traffic citations.

The Jury

While juries in criminal cases may consist of as few as six members, the most common jury composition in criminal cases is of twelve members. Jurors are selected from a jury pool. The jury pool is formed by selecting (usually randomly) potential jurors from a list created by listing citizens who live within the geographical jurisdiction of the court. Different jurisdictions do this in different ways. Some prepare lists from voter registration records, motor vehicle registration records, property tax rolls, and so forth. Members of the jury pool must report for jury duty on a specified date and time. When a case is scheduled for trial, each juror in the pool is assigned a number, and the first slate of potential jurors is randomly selected by number.

Jury Selection Process

The Sixth Amendment stipulates that juries must be impartial. In order to eliminate those jurors who might be biased, the court conducts a *voir dire* examination. Voir Dire is the process of questioning potential jurors and possibly eliminating some of them. In most state courts, both the prosecution and defense may eliminate potential jurors. A **challenge for cause** can be made if it is demonstrated that the juror is biased in some way. Some jurisdictions allow a certain number of **peremptory challenges**. A peremptory challenge is the disqualification of a potential juror from jury service where no reason for the challenge is stated. The lawyers are prohibited, however, from excluding anyone from jury duty based on race or gender. This is very difficult to enforce in practice since nearly any reason, no matter how trivial, can be offered to explain why a particular individual was excluded.

Elements of a Trial

Going forward to a trial is serious business for the defendant. If the prosecution is willing to go that far, then they are convinced that they have a compelling case against the defendant. Statistics show that most criminal defendants that take their case to trial will be found guilty.

Opening Statements

A criminal trial begins with both sides making statements to the jury. Generally, each side will make statements about what they intend to prove. As a matter of legal custom, the prosecution goes first because it has the *burden of proof*. The opening statements are not supposed to be argumentative in nature. Both sides in the case are required to limit their comments to the facts and evidence that will be presented. In practice, lawyers will often infuse elements of argumentation and dramatic flair into their opening remarks. The idea of the opening statements is to provide a "road map" of the case to the jury.

The Role of Evidence

Facts asserted by both sides in a criminal trial must be supported by evidence. There are several types of evidence. **Testimonial evidence** consists of statements made by anyone with knowledge of an event. **Direct evidence** is evidence that tends to prove directly a fact in question. **Circumstantial evidence** is evidence that creates an inference that a fact exists. Recall that the burden of proof in a criminal case is on the prosecution. Technically, the defense does not have to prove anything to prevail. Most defense attorneys, however, will present evidence to counter the evidence presented by the prosecution.

Hearsay is not generally admissible in court, but there are many exceptions to the hearsay rule. Hearsay is testimony given when the person testifying has no direct knowledge of the facts. In other words, it is second-hand information. One of the most commonly referenced exceptions to the hearsay rule is the *dying declaration*. A dying declaration is a statement made by a person that believes that they are about to die. The logic of this exception is that people who are about to die have no reason to lie, and that truthfulness can be safely assumed. The procedural rules for the admission of evidence at trial are complex. The courts have heavily regulated what evidence can be presented and how it can be presented in a long history of decisions, as well as **rules of evidence**. Federal courts abide by the **federal rules of evidence**, which are a codified version of the rules that developed over hundreds of years from the common law tradition.

The Prosecution's Case

The next phase of a trial after the prosecution and defense has presented opening statements is the presentation of the state's evidence by the prosecutor. The prosecutor will call witnesses and conduct direct examinations. The defense is permitted to conduct cross-examinations of the witnesses to discredit their testimony. This courtroom testimony is mandatory because the Sixth Amendment guarantees criminal defendants the right to face and question those who give evidence against them. This is often known as the **confrontation clause**.

The Defense's Case

As a legal matter, there is no requirement that the defense present any evidence. The burden of proof is on the prosecutor. In other words, the defense is under no obligation to prove innocence. All the defense needs to do to prevail is to show that prosecution failed to prove every element of the offense *beyond a reasonable doubt*. This is no easy task; the beyond the reasonable doubt standard is the highest standard of proof known to American law. Because of the Fifth Amendment protection, the defendant cannot be compelled to testify. Whether or not the defendant does testify is a matter of defense strategy. If the defendant does testify, he or she must face cross-examination.

The most important job of the defense attorney then is the creation of reasonable doubt in the minds of the jurors. This can be done using several strategies. Perhaps the most obvious defense strategy is to present an **alibi**. Another common strategy is to provide a different account from the prosecution of the evidence that links the defendant to the crime. Another tactic is to attack the credibility and competence of the prosecution's witnesses.

Closing Arguments

The **closing arguments** provide each side the opportunity to summarize the evidence presented, and clarify the opposing theories as to what happened. The lawyers are limited to talking about the evidence that has already been presented, and cannot introduce new evidence or refer to evidence that was not presented. Judges will usually inform the attorneys of his decisions regarding the jury instructions prior to this phase. Knowing what the instructions will be, the attorneys can use the closing argument to relate the instructions to specific pieces of evidence. In a criminal matter, the prosecution usually will present closing arguments first. The Defense attorney will then give closing arguments for the defense, and will usually speak to the statement made by the prosecutor in the State's closing arguments. In many jurisdictions, the prosecution is allowed a final speech before the jury, known as a **rebuttal**.

Jury Instructions

Before the jury leaves the courtroom to deliberate, the judge will give them what are known as **jury instructions**. These include the elements of the offense charged, how they should apply facts to the law, and defines pertinent legal concepts such as beyond a reasonable doubt. Possible verdicts are usually part of the jury instructions. The basic idea is to provide the jury with the relevant law that they should consider in their deliberations. Because the jury instructions must meet certain legal requirements and may be grounds for later appeals, judges often read the instructions to the jury verbatim. This reading of the instructions is known as the judge's **charge** to the jury.

Jury Deliberations

After the jury has been charged, the jurors will retire to a jury room for deliberations. The first order of business is to elect a **foreperson**. The foreperson will preside over the jury deliberations, and deliver the jury's final verdict. Jury deliberations are conducted in secret, and a bailiff will usually be assigned to ensure that no one communicates with the jury during deliberations. If the jury does not reach a verdict by the end of the first day of deliberations, it may be **sequestered**. *Sequestration* means moving the jurors to a place where they will be secluded and compelled to avoid contact with people and media that might result in the jurors obtaining information about the case. In most cases, the jurors are simply allowed to go home for the night and instructed not to read newspapers, watch news programs, or discuss the case.

Most states require that the final verdict reached by a jury in a criminal trial be unanimous. A jury that cannot reach a unanimous verdict is known as a **hung jury**. If the jury hangs, the judge has no choice but to dismiss the case. If the case is dismissed because of a hung jury, the prosecutor has the option to retry the case in front of a new jury. If however, the jury finds the defendant not guilty, then the same government cannot try the person again for the same charges. This prohibition against trying a person twice for the same offense is known as **double jeopardy**. The Fifth Amendment prohibition against double jeopardy does not, however, prohibit the person from being sued in civil court, or being charged with the offense by another government entity, such as another state or the federal government.

The Jury Decision in Capital Cases

The death penalty is such a serious punishment that those faced with it are given certain extra procedural safeguards. In capital cases, the trial is said to be bifurcated, or split into two parts. The first part of the trial requires the jury to determine guilt or innocence, and the second part of the trial asks jurors to determine if the person deserves to be executed for his (or very rarely her) crimes. In such bifurcated proceedings, the proceedings move to the penalty phase only after a guilty verdict has been reached. During the penalty phase, the jurors hear about **aggravating circumstances** and **mitigating circumstances**. Aggravating circumstances are things that make the crime more offensive to the public, such as when the victim of a murder is a child or a police officer. Mitigating circumstances, on the other hand, are things that make the defendant less culpable for his or her crimes. If the jury cannot unanimously agree on the death penalty, then most jurisdictions have legislation that provides for an automatic life sentence.

Jury Nullification

As a matter of legal theory, the American system of justice proceeds under the rule of law. In a perfect world, the laws would be completely just, the agents of the criminal justice system would be impartial, and sentences would always be proportional to the offense. In reality, juries can take issue with the substance of the law, the administration of the law, or the sentence imposed by the law. When juries are dissatisfied in this way, they can sometimes disregard the letter of the law and acquit the defendant despite evidence that reaches the level of proof beyond a reasonable doubt. This disregard of the law by jurors is known as **jury nullification**.

The Posttrial Process

In most jurisdictions, the jury serves as a finder of fact, and are done with their service when a verdict is returned. If that verdict is guilty, the judge most often imposes sentence. Some jurisdictions, however, use a bifurcated trial system where the jury participates in a sentencing phase and chooses the sentence.

Posttrial Motions

After a guilty verdict is handed down and a sentence is imposed, the defense can still file a few motions. With any guilty verdict, the defense can file a motion for a new trial. If the trial judge sustains this motion, a there will be a new trial, starting from scratch.

Key Terms

Aggravating Circumstances, Alibi, Bifurcated Trial, Challenge for Cause, Charge to the Jury, Circumstantial Evidence, Closing Arguments, Confrontation Clause, Direct Evidence, Double Jeopardy, Federal Rules of Evidence, Foreperson, Hearsay, Hung Jury, Jury Instructions, Jury Nullification, Mitigating Circumstances, Motion for a New Trial, Peremptory Challenge, Rebuttal, Right to a Public Trial, Right to a Speedy Trial, Right to a Trial by Jury, Right to Confront Witnesses, Right to Notice of Accusations, Rules of Evidence, Sequester, Testimonial Evidence, *Voir Dire*

Section 5.5: Sentencing

Learning Objectives

After completing this section, you should be able to:

5.5(a) Recite the text of the Eighth Amendment, and discuss the impact of each clause on the American criminal justice system.
5.5(b) Describe the differences between structured and indeterminate sentencing.
5.5(c) Describe the different types of structured sentences in use today.
5.5(d) Trace the historical reasons for the development of mandatory sentencing laws.
5.5(e) Describe the content and function of a presentence investigation report.
5.5(f) Trace the history and describe the function of the federal sentencing guidelines.
5.5(g) Outline the major arguments for and against the death penalty.

Introduction

In most jurisdictions, the judge holds the responsibility of imposing criminal sentences on convicted offenders. Often, this is a difficult process that defines the application of simple sentencing principles. The latitude that a judge has in imposing sentences can vary widely from state to state. This is because state legislatures often set the minimum and maximum punishments for particular crimes in criminal statutes. The law also specifies alternatives to incarceration that a judge may use to tailor a sentence to an individual offender.

Presentence Investigation

Many jurisdictions require that a presentence investigation take place before a sentence is handed down. Most of the time, the presentence investigation is conducted by a probation officer, and results in a **presentence investigation report**. This document describes the convict's education, employment record, criminal history, present offense, prospects for rehabilitation, and any personal issues, such as addiction, that may impact the court's decision. The report usually contains a recommendation as to the sentence that the court should impose. These reports are a major influence on the judge's final decision.

Victim Impact Statements

Many states now consider the impact that a crime had on the victim when determining an appropriate sentence. A few states even allow the victims to appear in court and testify. **Victim impact statements** are usually read aloud in open court during the sentencing phase of a trial. Criminal defendants have challenged the constitutionality of this process on the grounds that it violates the **Proportionality Doctrine** requirement of the Eighth Amendment, but the Supreme Court has rejected this argument and found the admission of victim statements constitutional.

The Sentencing Hearing

Many jurisdictions pass final sentences in a phase of the trial process known as a **sentencing hearing**. The prosecutor will recommend a sentence in the name of the people, or defend the recommended sentence in the presentence investigation report, depending on the jurisdiction. Defendants retain the right to counsel during this phase of the process. Defendants also have the right to make a statement to the judge before the sentence is handed down.

Influences on Sentencing Decisions

The severity of a sentence usually hinges on two major factors. The first is the seriousness of the offense. The other, which is much more complex, is the presence of aggravating or mitigating circumstances. In general the more serious the crime, the harsher the punishment.

Concurrent versus Consecutive Sentences

It is not uncommon for a person to be indicted on multiple offenses. This can be several different offenses, or a repetition of the same offense. In many jurisdictions, the judge has the option to order the sentences to be served **concurrently** or **consecutively**. A concurrent sentence means that the sentences are served at the same time. A consecutive sentence means that the defendant serves the sentences one after another.

Types of Sentences

A **sentence** is the punishment ordered by the court for a convicted defendant. Statutes usually prescribe punishments at both the state and federal level. The most important limit on the severity of punishments in the United States is the Eighth Amendment.

The Death Penalty

The death penalty is a sentencing option in thirty-eight states and the federal government. It is usually reserved for those convicted of murders with aggravating circumstances. Because of the severity and irrevocability of the death penalty, its use has heavily circumscribed by statutes and controlled by case law. Included among these safeguards is an automatic review by appellate courts.

Incarceration

The most common punishment after fines in the United States is the deprivation of liberty known as *incarceration*. *Jails* are short-term facilities, most often run by counties under the auspices of the sheriff's department. Jails house those awaiting trial and unable to make bail, and convicted offenders serving short sentences or waiting on a bed in a prison. *Prisons* are long-term facilities operated by state and federal governments. Most prison inmates are felons serving sentences of longer than one year.

Probation

Probation serves as a middle ground between no punishment and incarceration. Convicts receiving probation are supervised within the community, and must abide by certain rules and restrictions. If they violate the conditions of their probation, they can have their probation revoked and can be sent to prison. Common conditions of probation include obeying all laws, paying fines and restitution as ordered by the court, reporting to a probation officer, not associating with criminals, not using drugs, submitting to searches, and submitting to drug tests.

The heavy use of probation is controversial. When the offense is nonviolent, the offender is not dangerous to the community, and the offender is willing to make restitution, then many agree that probation is a good idea. Due to prison overcrowding, judges have been forced to place more and more offenders on probation rather than sentencing them to prison.

Intensive Supervision Probation (ISP)

Intensive Supervision Probation (ISP) is similar to standard probation, but requires much more contact with probation officers and usually has more rigorous conditions of probation. The primary focus of adult ISP is to provide protection of the public safety through close supervision of the offender. Many juvenile programs, and an increasing number of adult programs, also have a treatment component that is designed to reduce recidivism.

Boot Camps

Convicts, often young men, sentenced to **boot camps** live in a military style environment complete with barracks and rigorous physical training. These camps usually last from three to six months, depending on the particular program. The core ideas of boot camp programs are to teach wayward youths discipline and accountability. While a popular idea among some reformers, the research shows little to no impact on recidivism.

House Arrest and Electronic Monitoring

The Special Curfew Program was the federal courts' first use of home confinement. It was part of an experimental program–a cooperative venture of the Bureau of Prisons, the U.S. Parole Commission, and the federal probation system–as an alternative to Bureau of Prisons Community Treatment Center (CTC) residence for eligible inmates. These inmates, instead of CTC placement, received parole dates advanced a maximum of 60 days and were subject to a curfew and minimum weekly contact with a probation officer. **Electronic monitoring** became part of the home confinement program several years later. In 1988, a pilot program was launched in two districts to evaluate the use of electronic equipment to monitor persons in the curfew program. The program was expanded nationally in 1991 and grew to include offenders on probation and supervised release and defendants on pretrial supervision as those who may be eligible to be placed on home confinement with electronic monitoring (Courts, 2015).

Today, most jurisdictions stipulate that offenders sentenced to house arrest must spend all or most of the day in their own homes. The popularity of house arrest has increased in recent years due to monitoring technology that allows a transmitter to be placed on the convict's ankle, allowing compliance to be remotely monitored. House arrest is often coupled with other sanctions, such as fines and community service. Some jurisdictions have a work requirement, where the offender on house arrest is allowed to leave home for a specified window of time in order to work.

Fines

Fines are very common for violations and minor misdemeanor offenses. First time offenders found guilty of simple assaults, minor drug possession, traffic violations and so forth are sentenced to fines alone. If these fines are not paid according to the rules set by the court, the offender is jailed. Many critics argue that fines discriminate against the poor. A $200 traffic fine means very little to a highly paid professional, but can be a serious burden on a college student with only a part-time job. Some jurisdictions use a sliding scale that bases fines on income known as **day fines**. They are an outgrowth of traditional fining systems, which were seen as disproportionately punishing offenders with modest means while imposing no more than "slaps on the wrist" for affluent offenders.

This system has been very popular in European countries such as Sweden and Germany. Day fines take the financial circumstances of the offender into account. They are calculated using two major factors: The seriousness of the offense and the offender's daily income. The European nations that use this system have established guidelines that assign points ("fine units") to different offenses based on the seriousness of the offense. The range of fine units varies greatly by country. For example, in Sweden the range is from 1 to 120 units. In Germany, the range is from 1 to 360 units.

The most common process is for court personnel to determine the daily income of the offender. It is common for family size and certain other expenses to be taken into account.

Restitution

When an offender is sentenced to a fine, the money goes to the state. *Restitution* requires the offender to pay money to the victim. The idea is to replace the economic losses suffered by the victim because of the crime. Judges may order offenders to compensate victims for medical bills, lost wages, and the value of property that was stolen or destroyed. The major problem with restitution is actually collecting the money on behalf of the victim. Some jurisdictions allow practices such as wage garnishment to ensure the integrity of the process. Restitution can also be made a condition of probation, whereby the offender is imprisoned for a probation violation is the restitution is not paid.

Community Service

As a matter of legal theory, crimes harm the entire community, not just the immediate victim. Advocates see community service as the violator paying the community back for the harm caused. **Community service** can include a wide variety of tasks such as picking up trash along roadways, cleaning up graffiti, and cleaning up parks. Programs based on community service have been popular, but little is known about the impact of these programs on recidivism rates.

"Scarlet-letter" Punishments

While exact practices vary widely, the idea of **scarlet-letter punishments** is to shame the offender. Advocates view shaming as a cheap and satisfying alternative to incarceration. Critics argue that criminals are not likely to mend their behavior because of shame. There are legal challenges that of kept this sort of punishment from being widely accepted. Appeals have been made because such punishments violate the Eighth Amendment ban on cruel and unusual punishment. Others have been based on the idea that they violate the First Amendment by compelling defendants to convey a judicially scripted message in the form of forced apologies, warning signs, newspaper ads, and sandwich boards. Still other appeals have been based on the notion that shaming punishments are not specifically authorized by State sentencing guidelines and therefore constitute an abuse of judicial discretion (Litowitz, 1997).

Asset Forfeiture

Many jurisdictions have laws that allow the government to seize property and assets used in criminal enterprises. Such a seizure is known as **forfeiture**. Automobiles, airplanes, and boats used in illegal drug smuggling are all subject to seizure. The assets are often given over to law enforcement. According to the FBI, "Many criminals are motivated by greed and the acquisition of material goods. Therefore, the ability of the government to forfeit property connected with criminal activity can be an effective law enforcement tool by reducing the incentive for illegal conduct. Asset forfeiture takes the profit out of crime by helping to eliminate the ability of the offender to command resources necessary to continue illegal activities" (FBI, 2015).

Asset forfeiture can be both a criminal and a civil matter. Civil forfeitures are easier on law enforcement because they do not require a criminal conviction. As a civil matter, the standard of proof is much lower than it would be if the forfeiture was a criminal penalty. Commonly, the standard for such a seizure is probable cause. With criminal asset forfeitures, law enforcement cannot take control of the assets until the suspect has been convicted in criminal court.

Appeals

An *appeal* is a claim that some procedural or legal error was made in the prior handling of the case. An appeal results in one of two outcomes. If the appellate court agrees with the lower court, then the appellate court **affirms** the lower court's decision. In such cases the appeals court is said to **uphold** the decision of the lower court. If the appellate court agrees with the plaintiff that an error occurred, then the appellate court will **overturn** the conviction. This happens only when the error is determined to be substantial. Trivial or insignificant errors will result in the appellate court affirming the decision of the lower court. Winning an appeal is rarely a "get out of jail free" card for the defendant. Most often, the case is **remanded** to the lower court for rehearing. The decision to retry the case ultimately rests with the prosecutor. If the decision of the appellate court requires the exclusion of important evidence, the prosecutor may decide that a conviction is not possible.

Sentencing Statutes and Guidelines

In the United States, most jurisdictions hold that criminal sentencing is entirely a matter of statute. That is, legislative bodies determine the punishments that are associated with particular crimes. These legislative assemblies establish such sentencing schemes by passing **sentencing statutes** or establishing *sentencing guidelines*. These sentences can be of different types that have a profound effect on both the administration of criminal justice and the life of the convicted offender.

Indeterminate Sentences

Indeterminate sentencing is a type of criminal sentencing where the convict is not given a sentence of a certain period in prison. Rather, the amount of time served is based on the offender's conduct while incarcerated. Most often, a broad range is specified during sentencing, and then a parole board will decide when the offender has earned release.

Determinate Sentences

A **determinate sentence** is of a fixed length, and is generally not subject to review by a parole board. Convicts must serve all of the time sentenced, minus any **good time** earned while incarcerated.

Mandatory Sentences

Mandatory sentences are a type of sentence where the absolute minimum sentence is established by a legislative body. This effectively limits judicial discretion in such cases. Mandatory sentences are often included in habitual offender laws, such as repeat drug offenders. Under federal law, prosecutors have the powerful plea bargaining tool of agreeing not to file under the prior felony statute.

Sentencing Guidelines

The **Sentencing Reform Act of 1984** was passed in response to congressional concern about fairness in federal sentencing practices. The Act completely changed the way courts sentenced federal offenders. The Act created a new federal agency, the U.S. Sentencing Commission, to set sentencing guidelines for every federal offense. When federal sentencing guidelines went into effect in 1987, they significantly altered judges' sentencing discretion, probation officers' preparation of the presentence investigation report, and officers' overall role in the sentencing process. The new sentencing scheme also placed officers in a more adversarial environment in the courtroom, where attorneys might dispute facts, question guideline calculations, and object to the information in the presentence report. In addition to providing for a new sentencing process, the Act also replaced parole with "supervised release," a term of community supervision to be served by prisoners after they completed prison terms (Courts, 2015).

When the Federal Courts began using sentencing guidelines, about half of the states adopted the practice. Sentencing guidelines indicate to the sentencing judge a narrow range of expected punishments for specific offenses. The purpose of these guidelines is to limit judicial discretion in sentencing. Several sentencing guidelines use a grid system, where the severity of the offense runs down one axis, and the criminal history of the offender runs across the other. The more serious the offense, the longer the sentence the offender receives. The longer the criminal history of the offender, the longer the sentence imposed. Some systems allow judges to go outside of the guidelines when *aggravating* or *mitigating* circumstances exist.

Key Terms

Asset Forfeiture, Boot Camps, Community Service, Concurrent Sentence, Consecutive Sentence, Day Fine, Death Penalty, Determinate Sentencing, Electronic Monitoring, Fine, Forfeiture, Good Time, Home Confinement, House Arrest, Indeterminate Sentencing, Intensive Supervision Probation (ISP), Mandatory Sentences, Overturn, Presentence Investigation Report, Proportionality Doctrine, Remand, Scarlet-Letter Punishments, Sentencing, Sentencing Hearing, Sentencing Reform Act of 1984, Sentencing Statute, U.S. Sentencing Commission, Uphold, Victim Impact Statement

Chapter 6: Prisons, Jails, and Community Corrections

In the grand scheme of the history of criminal justice, the idea of incarceration as punishment is a relatively new idea. Those who violated ancient laws were sentenced to **corporal punishments**, fines, and death. The first modern prisons began in the eighteenth century when the Quakers, motivated by religious altruism, devised them as an alternative to corporal and capital punishment. The intent of these reformers was to rehabilitate offenders through hard physical labor, religious study, and **penitence**. The contemporary political climate has largely replaced these altruistic ideas with the ideas of *deterrence, retribution*, and *incapacitation.*

Unfortunately, the **prison industrial complex** is a growth industry, and efforts at reducing the number of Americans in confinement have met with only marginal success. Elected officials, eager to demonstrate a tough stance against crime to the public, have created harsh sentencing laws that have filled existing prisons over capacity, and have spawned the building of many new prisons. The financial costs of this have been staggering.

The trend of American incarceration seems to be continuing downward. In 2012, the number of admissions to state and federal prison in the United States was 609,800 offenders, the lowest number since 1999. The number of releases from U.S. prisons in 2012 (637,400) exceeded that of admissions for the fourth consecutive year, contributing to the decline in the total U.S. prison population. Many reform-minded critics argue that most prisoners are locked up on drug charges, but the statistics do not support this view. In 2011, the majority of state prisoners (53%) were serving time for violent offenses. This downward trend is not encouraging considering the size of the problem to begin with. At yearend 2012, about 6.94 million people were supervised by the U.S. adult correctional systems, which was the equivalent to about 1 in 35 U.S. adults. On the brighter side, this was the lowest rate observed since 1997.

Not all of these numbers represent prisoners in state prisons. In 2012, about 3.94 million offenders were supervised in the community on probation and 851,200 on parole. Around 1.35 million were incarcerated in state prisons, 217,800 in federal prisons and 744,500 in local jails. The largest jurisdictions account for a disproportionate amount of those under confinement or supervision. The federal prison system had the largest sentenced prison population (196,600 inmates) in 2012, followed by Texas (157,900), California (134,200), Florida (101,900) and New York (54,100).

Section 6.1: Jails

Learning Objectives

After completing this section, you should be able to:

6.1(a) Describe the purposes of jails in the United States today.
6.1(b) Identify some of the issues faced by jail administrators today.
6.1(c) Describe the administrative structure of the typical American jail.
6.1(d) Describe the various types of inmates that jail staff must supervise.
6.1(e) List and describe the various types of facilities that detain juveniles.

Introduction

The idea of jails has a long history, and the historical roots of American jails are in the "gaols" of feudal England. Sheriffs operated these early jails, and their primary purpose was to hold accused persons awaiting trial. This English model was brought over to the Colonies, but the function remained the same. In the 1800s, jails began to change in response to the penitentiary movement. Their function was extended to housing those convicted of minor offenses and sentenced to short terms of incarceration. They were also used for other purposes, such as holding the mentally ill and vagrants. The advent of a separate juvenile justice system and the development of state hospitals alleviated the burden of taking care of these later categories.

Today's jails are critical components of local criminal justice systems. They are used to address the need for secure detention at various points in the criminal justice process. Jails typically serve several law enforcement agencies in the community, including local law enforcement, state police, wildlife conservation officers, and federal authorities. Jails respond to many needs in the criminal justice system and play an integral role within every tier of American criminal justice. These needs are ever changing and influenced by the policies, practices, and philosophies of the many different users of the jail. Running a jail is a tough business, usually undertaken by a county sheriff. Often, much of the Sheriff's authority is delegated to a jail administrator.

Running a jail is such a complicated endeavor partly because jails serve an extremely diverse population. Unlike prisons where inmate populations are somewhat homogenous, fails hold vastly different individuals. Jails hold both men and women, and both children and adults. Most state prisoners are serious offenders, whereas jails old both serious offenders as well as minor offenders who may be vulnerable to predatory criminals. Those suffering from mental illness, alcoholism, and drug addiction often find themselves in jail. It is in this environment that jail staff must accomplish the two major functions of jails: Intake and Custody.

Booking and Intake

The booking and intake function of jails serves a vital public safety function by providing a secure environment in which potentially dangerous persons can be assessed, and the risk these individuals pose the public can be determined.

Custody

The second major function of jails is the idea of custody. That is, people are deprived of their liberty for various reasons. The two most common of these reasons are *pretrial detention* and *punishment.*

Pretrial Detention

A major use of modern jails is what is often referred to as **pretrial detention**. In other words, jails receive accused persons pending arraignment and hold them awaiting trial, conviction, or sentencing. More than half of jail inmates are accused of crimes and are awaiting trial. The average time between arrest and sentencing is around six months. Jails also readmit probation and parole violators and absconders, holding them for judicial hearings. The major purpose of pretrial detention is not to punish offenders, but to protect the public and ensure the appearance of accused persons at trial.

According to the Bureau of Justice Statistics, there are around 3,300 jails currently in operation within the United States. This large number points to a very important fact: Jails are primarily a local concern. **Jails** (and **detention centers**) are facilities designed to safely and securely hold a variety of criminal offenders, usually for a short period. The wide variety of offenders comes from the fact that jails have dual roles. They hold criminal defendants waiting on processing by the criminal justice system, and they hold those convicted of crimes and sentenced to a jail term. In addition, jails hold prisoners for other agencies, such as state departments of correction, until bed space becomes available in a state prison.

The size of jails can vary widely depending on the jurisdiction the facility serves. Both geographic and legal jurisdiction must be considered. The single most important determinant of jail size is population density. The more people a given jurisdiction has, the more jail inmates they are likely to have. Many rural jails are quite small, but America's largest population centers tend to have massive jail complexes. Most counties and many municipalities operate jails, and a few are operated by federal and other non-local agencies. There has been a trend for small, rural jurisdictions to combine their jails into regional detention facilities. These consolidated operations can increase efficiency, security, and better ensure prisoners' rights.

Punishment

A primary function of jails is to house criminal defendants after arrest. Within a very narrow window of time, the arrestee must appear before a judge. The judge will consider the charges against the defendant and the defendant's risk of flight when determining bail. The judge may decide to remand the defendant to the custody of the jail until trial, but this is rare. Most often, pretrial release will be granted. The arrestees may be required to pay a certain amount of money to ensure their appearance in court, or they may be released on their own recognizance.

As a criminal sanctioning option, jails provide a method of holding offenders accountable for criminal acts. Jails house offenders that have been sentenced to a jail term for misdemeanor offenses, usually for less than one year. There are many ways that jail sentences can be served, depending largely on the laws and policies of the particular jurisdiction. A central goal of incarceration as punishment in the criminal justice system is the philosophical goal of *deterrence.* Many believe that jail sentences discourage offenders from committing future criminal acts (specific deterrence) and to potential criminals about the possible costs of crime (general deterrence). Rehabilitation and reintegration are sometimes considered secondary goals of incarceration. These goals are not usually deemed amenable to the jail environment, and few programs designed to meet these goals exist. Many local jails do make a modest effort to provide inmates with opportunities for counseling and change to deter future criminal behavior, but always within the constraints of scant resources.

Miscellaneous Functions

Jails in some jurisdictions are responsible for transferring and transporting inmates to federal, state, or other authorities. Jails are also tasked with holding mentally ill persons pending their transfer to suitable mental health facilities where beds are often unavailable. Jails also hold people for a variety of government purposes; they hold individuals wanted by the armed forces, for protective custody of individuals who may not be safe in the community, for those found in contempt of court, and witnesses for the courts. Jails often hold state and federal inmates due to overcrowding in prison facilities. Jails are commonly tasked with community-based sanctions, such as work details engaged in public services.

Jail Populations

Arrestees often arrive at the jail with myriad many problems. Substance abuse, alcohol abuse, and mental illness often mean that jail inmates are not amenable to complying with the directions of jail staff. Many have medical problems, psychological problems, and emotional problems. Inmates can display the full gambit of human emotions: fail staff may see fear, anxiety, anger, and depression every day. Behaviors often mirror emotional state, and at times staff must deal with noncompliant, suicidal, or violent inmates. While inmates are in custody, the jail is responsible for their health and wellbeing.

Jails function in a role as a service provider for the rest of the criminal justice community. Jail administrators have very little discretion in who goes to jail and how long they remain in custody. Law and policy play a big role in dictating who goes to jail, as do the discretionary decisions of probation and parole officers, law enforcement, and judges. Prevalent community attitudes are also important, because voters can place pressure on law enforcement and the courts to make more arrests and prosecute more offenders. When this happens, more people end up in jail.

Juvenile Detention

Many jails temporarily detain juveniles pending transfer to juvenile authorities.

Recent research by the Office of Juvenile Justice and Delinquency Prevention (OJJDP) shows that the trend in juvenile incarceration is toward lower numbers and a move toward local facilities. The juvenile offender population dropped 14% from 2010 to 2012, to the lowest number since 1975. In the March 2015 report, it was noted that for the first time since 2000, more offenders were in local facilities than were in state operated facilities.

The degree of security present in juvenile facilities tends to vary widely between jurisdictions. An important measure of security used in OJJDP reports is locking youth in "sleeping rooms." Recent data indicates that public agencies are far more likely to lock juveniles in their sleeping quarters at least some of the time. A majority of state agencies (61%) reported engaging in this practice, while only a relatively small number (11%) of private agencies reported this practice. More than half of all facilities reported that they had one or more confinement features in addition to locking juveniles in their sleeping room (which usually happens at night). These security features usually consist of locked doors and gates designed to keep juveniles within the facility.

Unlike adult jails, juvenile detention takes place in a variety of different environments. According to the OJJDP study, the most common type of facility were facilities that considered themselves to be "residential treatment centers," followed by those that considered themselves to be "detention centers." The classifications of "group home," "training school," "shelter," "wilderness camp," and "diagnostic center" are also used. Group homes and shelters tended to be privately owned, and detention centers tended to be state run facilities.

Key Terms

Corporal Punishment, Custody, Detention Centers, Detention Facility, Diagnostic Center, Gaol, Group Home, Intake, Juvenile Detention Center, Office of Juvenile Justice and Delinquency Prevention (OJJDP), Penitence, Prison Industrial Complex, Residential Treatment Center, Shelter, Training School, Wilderness Camp

Section 6.2: Prisons

Learning Objectives

After completing this section, you should be able to:

6.2(a) Describe the purposes of today's prisons.
6.2(b) Describe the size and characteristics of the prison population in the United States today.
6.2(c) Explain the ideas of "just deserts" and "get tough on crime" policies and how they impacted prison populations.
6.2(d) Trace the development of modern prisons, identifying key reformers.
6.2(e) Identify the characteristics of institutions based on their security level.

Introduction

As inmates enter a prison system after sentencing, they are typically assessed at a classification or reception facility based on the nature of their crime, criminal history, escape risk, health needs, and any behavioral issues that must be addressed. The goal of these assessments is to determine the dangerousness of the offender and the viability of various treatment options. Based on the assessment results, prison personnel will assign the offender to a particular prison facility. The primary concern when assigning an inmate to a facility is safety, followed by practical concerns about bed space. The needs of the inmate are also considered in the process. Prisoners thus have almost no control of where they are confined. Some prisons do allow for transfers to facilities closer to family, but these requests are subject to security concerns and bed space. Often, female inmates are housed far from family because the small number of female facilities often means that there are no options close to family.

Development of Modern Prisons

Prior to the 1800s, common law countries relied heavily on physical punishments. Influenced by the high ideas of the enlightenment, reformers began to move the criminal justice system away from physical punishments in favor of reforming offenders. This was a dramatic shift away from the mere infliction of pain that had prevailed for centuries. Among these early reformers was **John Howard**, who advocated the use of **penitentiaries**. Penitentiaries, as the name suggests, were places for offenders to be **penitent**. That is, they would engage in work and reflection on their misdeeds. To achieve the appropriate atmosphere for penitence, prisoners were kept in solitary cells with much time for reflection.

Philadelphia's **Walnut Street Jail** was an early effort to model the European penitentiaries. The system used there later became known as the Pennsylvania System. Under this system, inmates were kept in solitary confinement in small, dark cells. A key element of the Pennsylvania System is that no communications whatsoever were allowed. Critics of this system began to speak out against the practice of solitary confinement early on. They maintained that the isolated conditions were emotionally damaging to inmates, causing severe distress and even mental breakdowns. Nevertheless, prisons across the United States began adopting the Pennsylvania model, espousing the value of rehabilitation.

The New York system evolved along similar lines, starting with the opening of New York's Auburn Penitentiary in 1819. This facility used what came to be known as the **congregate system**. Under this system, inmates spent their nights in individual cells, but were required to congregate in workshops during the day. Work was serious business, and inmates were not allowed to talk while on the job or at meals. This emphasis on labor has been associated with the values that accompanied the Industrial Revolution. By the middle of the nineteenth century, prospects for the penitentiary movement were grim. No evidence had been mustered to suggest that penitentiaries had any real impact on rehabilitation and recidivism.

Prisons in the South and West were quite different from those in the Northeast. In the Deep South, the **lease system** developed. Under the lease system, businesses negotiated with the state to exchange convict labor for the care of the inmates. Prisoners were primarily used for hard, manual labor, such as logging, cotton picking, and railroad construction. Eastern ideas of penology did not catch on in the West, with the exception of California. Prior to statehood, many frontier prisoners were held in federal military prisons.

Disillusionment with the penitentiary idea, combined with overcrowding and understaffing, led to deplorable prison conditions across the country by the middle of the nineteenth century. New York's Sing Sing Prison was a noteworthy example of the brutality and corruption of that time. A new wave of reform achieved momentum in 1870 after a meeting of the National Prison Association (which would later become the American Correctional Association). At this meeting held in Cincinnati, members issued a Declaration of Principles. This document expressed the idea that prisons should be operated according to a philosophy that prisoners should be reformed, and that reform should be rewarded with release from confinement. This ushered in what has been called the **Reformatory Movement**.

One of the earliest prisons to adopt this philosophy was the **Elmira Reformatory**, which was opened in 1876 under the leadership of **Zebulon Brockway**. Brockway ran the reformatory in accordance with the idea that education was the key to inmate reform. Clear rules were articulated, and inmates that followed those rules were classified at higher levels of privilege. Under this "mark" system, prisoners earned marks (credits) toward release. The number of marks that an inmate was required to earn in order to be released was established according to the seriousness of the offense. This was a movement away from the doctrine of proportionality, and toward indeterminate sentences and community corrections.

The next major wave of corrections reform was known as the **rehabilitation model**, which achieved momentum during the 1930s. This era was marked by public favor with psychology and other social and behavioral sciences. Ideas of punishment gave way to ideas of treatment, and optimistic reformers began attempts to rectify social and intellectual deficiencies that were the proximate causes of criminal activity. This was essentially a **medical model** in which criminality was a sort of disease that could be cured. This model held sway until the 1970s when rising crime rates and a changing prison population undermined public confidence.

After the belief that "nothing works" became popular, the **crime control model** became the dominate paradigm of corrections in the United States. The model attacked the rehabilitative model as being "soft on crime." "Get tough" policies became the norm throughout the 1980s and 1990s, and lengthy prison sentences became common. The aftermath of this has been a dramatic increase in prison populations and a corresponding increase in corrections expenditures. Those expenditures have reached the point that many states can no longer sustain their departments of correction. The pendulum seems to be swinging back toward a rehabilitative model, with an emphasis on community corrections. While the community model has existed parallel to the crime control model for many years, it seems to be growing in prominence.

Prison Classifications

Prisons in the United States today are usually distinguished by **custody levels**. **Super-maximum-security prisons** are used to house the most violent and most escape prone inmates. These institutions are characterized by almost no inmate mobility within the facility, and fortress-like security measures. This type of facility is very expensive to build and operate. The first such prison was the notorious federal prison Alcatraz, built by the Federal Bureau of Prisons in 1934.

Maximum-security prisons are fortresses that house the most dangerous prisoners. Only 20% of the prisons in the United States are labeled as maximum security, but, because of their size, they hold about

33% of the inmates in custody. Because super-max prisons are relatively rare, maximum-security facilities hold the vast majority of America's dangerous convicts. These facilities are characterized by very low levels of inmate mobility, and extensive physical security measures. Tall walls and fences are common features, usually topped with razor wire. Watchtowers staffed by officers armed with rifles are common as well. Security lighting and video cameras are almost universal features.

States that use the death penalty usually place **death row** inside a maximum-security facility. These areas are usually segregated from the general population, and extra security measures are put in place. Death row is often regarded as a prison within a prison, often having different staff and procedures than the rest of the facility.

Medium-security prisons use a series of fences or walls to hold prisoners that, while still considered dangerous, are less of a threat than maximum-security prisoners. The physical security measures placed in these facilities is often as tight as for maximum-security institutions. The major difference is that medium-security facilities offer more inmate mobility, which translates into more treatment and work options. These institutions are most likely to engage inmates in industrial work, such as the printing of license plates for the State.

Minimum-security prisons are institutions that usually do not have walls and armed security. Prisoners housed in minimum-security prisons are considered to be nonviolent and represent a very small escape risk. Most of these institutions have far more programs for inmates, both inside the prison and outside in the community. Part of the difference in inmate rights and privileges stems from the fact that most inmates in minimum-security facilities are "short timers." In other words, they are scheduled for release soon. The idea is to make the often problematic transition from prison to community go more smoothly. Inmates in these facilities may be assigned there initially, or they may have worked their way down from higher security levels through good behavior and an approaching release date.

Women are most often housed in **women's prisons**. These are distinguished along the same lines as male institutions. These institutions tend to be smaller than their male counterparts are, and there are far fewer of them. Women do not tend to be as violent as men are, and this is reflected in what they are incarcerated for. The majority of female inmates are incarcerated for drug offenses. Inmate turnover tends to be higher in women's prisons because they tend to receive shorter sentences.

A few states operate coeducational prisons where both male and female inmates live together. The reason for this is that administrators believe that a more normal social environment will better facilitate eventual reintegration of both sexes into society. The fear of predation by adult male offenders keeps most facilities segregated by gender.

In the recent past, the dramatic growth in prison populations led to the emergence of private prisons. Private organizations claimed that they could own and operate prisons more efficiently than government agencies can. The Corrections Corporation of America is the largest commercial operator of jails and prisons in the United States. The popularity of the idea has waned in recent years, mostly due to legal liability issues and a failure to realize the huge savings promised by the private corporations.

Special Populations

A major problem affecting the operation of prisons in the United States is what is known as **special populations**. Among these are elderly inmates. An aging population in general coupled with mandatory sentencing laws has caused an explosion in the number. This is an expensive proposition for the American correctional system. A substantial reason for this increased cost is the increased medical attention people tend to require as they grow older. Prisons that rely on prison industry to subsidize the cost of operations find that elderly inmates are less able to work than their younger counterparts. There is also the fear that younger inmates will prey on elderly ones. This phenomenon has caused the federal prison system and many state systems to rethink the policies that contribute to this "graying" of correctional populations.

Substantial growth has also been seen in the number of inmates that are ill. Arthritis and hypertension are the most commonly reported chronic conditions among inmates, but more serious and less easily treated maladies are also common. Many larger jails and prisons have special sections devoted to inmates with medical problems. In addition to the normal security staff, these units must employ medical staff. Recruiting medical staff that are willing to work in confinement with inmates is a constant problem for administrators.

According to many critics of mental health in America, the number of mentally ill inmates has reached crisis level. There has been explosive growth in the incarceration of mentally ill persons since the *deinstitutionalization* movement of the 1960s. As well-meaning people advocated for the rights of American's mentally ill, they fostered in a sinister unintended consequence: As mental hospitals closed, America's jails became the dumping ground for America's mentally ill population. This problem was exacerbated at the federal level by the passage of the Community Mental Health Act of 1963, which substantially reduced funding of mental health hospitals. With state hospitals gone or severely restricted, communities had to deal with the issue of what to do with mentally ill persons. Most communities responded with the poor solution of criminalizing the mentally ill.

Prison Overcrowding

While the trend in prison population data is down, prison overpopulation is still a major problem in many states. Many of those states are under court order to fix overcrowding problems, which are unconstitutional. Governments have responded with many programs aimed at reducing **prison overcrowding**. More prisons have been built, existing facilities have been retrofitted to house more inmates within legal guidelines, early release programs have been instituted, and the range of criminal sanctions beyond traditional parole and prison sentences has been implemented. Many states have altered the criminal laws to decriminalize or reduce the classification of crimes, in effect sending fewer people to prison.

Prison Programs

Prisons are like small cities in many respects. All of the requirements of life must be met, and rehabilitative objectives must be facilitated. Medical services must be rendered, and religious needs must be met. Inmates have a right to some types of recreation. Many prisons have labor and industry programs. Rehabilitative programs include job training, addiction treatment, therapy for psychological and emotional problems, and many other programs are common.

Key Terms

American Correctional Association, Congregate System, Crime Control Model, Custody Level, Death Row, Declaration of Principles, Elmira Reformatory, John Howard, Lease System, Maximum-security Prison, Medical Model, Medium-security Prison, Minimum-security Prison, Penitent, Penitentiary, Pennsylvania System, Prison Overcrowding, Prison Programs, Private Prisons, Reception Facility, Reformatory Movement, Rehabilitation Model, Special Populations, Super-maximum-security Prison, Walnut Street Jail, Women's Prisons, Zebulon Brockway

Section 6.3: Prisoner's Rights

Learning Objectives

After completing this section, you should be able to:

6.3(a)   Describe the consequences of major Supreme Court decisions about prisoner's rights on corrections administration.
6.3(b)   Explain the legal concept of a "state created liberty interest" in the context of prisoner's rights.
6.3(c)   Describe the various First Amendment rights of prisoners that the Court has protected, and which ones they have limited.
6.3(d)   List and describe the rights that prisoners have during prison disciplinary hearings.
6.3(e)   Describe how the Court has applied the Eighth Amendment to conditions inside prisons.

Introduction

American courts were reluctant to get involved in prison affairs during most of the 19th century. Until the 1960s, the courts used a hands-off approach to dealing with corrections. Since, it the court has recognized that "Prison walls do not form a barrier separating prison inmates from the protections of the Constitution" (Turner v. Safley, 1987). Prisoners do give up certain rights because of conviction, but not all of them. The high courts have established that prisoners retain certain constitutional rights. As the Court stated in *Hudson v. Palmer* (1984), "While prisoners enjoy many protections of the Constitution that are not fundamentally inconsistent with imprisonment itself or incompatible with the objectives of incarceration, imprisonment carries with it the circumscription or loss of many rights as being necessary to accommodate the institutional needs and objectives of prison facilities, particularly internal security and safety." From this statement, it can be seen that institutional safety and security will usually trump inmate rights when the two collide in Court.

Political Rights

The phrase **political right** is used to refer to rights related to the participation in the democracy of the United States. Chief among these is the right to vote. The Constitution of the United States allows states to revoke a person's right to vote upon conviction, but does not require it. Several states revoke the right to vote while a person is incarcerated, but restore the right once the person is released from prison. A few states revoke the right to vote for life when a person is convicted of a felony. The right to vote cannot be denied to those who are pretrial detainees confined to jail or a misdemeanant. These individuals are usually given the right to vote by absentee ballot.

The Right to Free Speech and Assembly

The First Amendment right of prisoners to free speech is curtailed, but not eliminated. Prison administrators must justify restrictions on free speech rights. The rights to assemble is generally curtailed. As a rule, prison administrators can ban any inmate activity that is a risk to the security and safety of the institution.

The Right to Freedom of Religion

Generally, prisoners have the right to free exercise of their religious beliefs. These, however, can be curtailed when the health and safety of the institution are at risk. To be protected, the particular religious beliefs must be "sincerely held." Prison officials may not, however, legally show preference for one religion over another. In practice, some religious customs have conflicted with prison policies, such as requiring work on religious holidays that forbid labor. These types of policies have been upheld by the courts.

The right of Access to the Courts

The First Amendment guarantees the right "to petition the Government for a redress of grievances." For prisoners, this has translated to certain types of access to the courts. The two major categories of petitions that can be filed by prisoners are criminal appeals (often by habeas corpus petitions) and civil rights lawsuits. The right to petition the courts in these ways is referred to as the **right of access to the courts**. The court discusses this right at length in the case of *Johnson v. Avery* (1969).

Freedom from Retaliation

Inmates who file complaints, grievances, and lawsuits against prison staff have a constitutional right to be free from retaliation. The Supreme Court based this right on the logic that retaliation by prison staff hampers the exercise of protected constitutional rights. In practice, this right has been difficult for inmates to assert. Prison staff can often find legitimate reasons for taking action that was intended as retaliation.

Rights During Prison Disciplinary Proceedings

In the landmark case of *Wolff v. McDonnell* (1974), the Supreme Court defined the contours of prisoner rights during prison disciplinary proceedings. While not all due process rights due a criminal defendant were due the prisoner in a disciplinary proceeding, some rights were preserved. Among those rights were:

- Advance written notice of charges must be given to the disciplinary action inmate, no less than 24 hours before his appearance before the Adjustment Committee.
- There must be a written statement by the factfinders as to the evidence relied on and reasons for the disciplinary action.
- The inmate should be allowed to call witnesses and present documentary evidence in his defense if permitting him to do so will not jeopardize institutional safety or correctional goals.
- The inmate has no constitutional right to confrontation and cross-examination in prison disciplinary proceedings, such procedures in the current environment, where prison disruption remains a serious concern, being discretionary with the prison officials.
- Inmates have no right to retained or appointed counsel.

The Right to Privacy

The right to privacy is closely related to the law of search and seizure. In the landmark case of *Hudson v. Palmer* (1984), the Court determined that inmates do not have a reasonable expectation of privacy in their living quarters. In the Court's rationale, the needs of institutional security outweigh the inmate's right to privacy. The policy implication of this decision is that **shakedowns** may be conducted at the discretion of prison staff, and no evidence of wrongdoing is necessary to justify the search.

The Right to Be Free From Cruel and Unusual Punishment

The right to be free from cruel and unusual punishment as guaranteed by the Eighth Amendment to the United States Constitution. The amendment only applies to criminal punishments; it has no bearing on civil cases.

Conditions in prison must not involve the "wanton and unnecessary" infliction of pain. Prison conditions, taken alone or in combination, may deprive inmates of the "minimal civilized measure of life's necessities." If this happens, the Court will judge the conditions of confinement unconstitutional. Conditions that cannot be said to be cruel and unusual under "contemporary standards" are not unconstitutional. According to the Court, prison conditions that are "restrictive and even harsh," are part of the penalty that criminal offenders pay for their "offenses against society" (*Rhodes v. Chapman*, 1981).

In *Estelle v. Gamble* (1976), the court ruled that "Deliberate indifference by prison personnel to a prisoner's serious illness or injury constitutes cruel and unusual punishment contravening the Eighth Amendment."

Key Terms

Estelle v. Gamble **(1976),** *Hudson v. Palmer* **(1984),** *Johnson v. Avery* **(1969), Political Right, Right to Access to the Courts, Right to Assemble, Right to be Free from Cruel and Unusual Punishment, Right to Free Speech, Right to the Free Exercise of Religion, Right to Vote, Shakedown,** *Wolff v. McDonnell* **(1974)**

Section 6.4: Parole, Probation, and Community Sanctions

Learning Objectives

6.4(a) Describe the advantages and disadvantages of probation.

6.4(b) Identify the major job duties of probation officers.

6.4(c) Identify the various sanctions that fall under the heading of community corrections.

6.4(d) Compare and contrast probation with parole.

6.4(e) Describe the concept of intermediate sanctions and describe programs that fall under that heading.

Introduction

Parole and probation, taken together with other forms of non-prison sanctions, are called **community corrections**. This is because these offenders reside in the community rather than in jail or prison. The idea of probation and parole is to reintroduce the offender into society as a productive member. The other major goal of probation and parole is to keep the community safe from predation.

Community-based sanctions are becoming increasingly popular as corrections budgets continue to rise, and overcrowding remains an issue. It is much cheaper to house an offender in the community than it is to keep them in prison. It is estimated that community supervision costs less than $1,000 per person supervised, while incarceration costs as much as $30,000 per prisoner. The push has been to increase prison time for predatory offenders, and to make room for them by finding alternatives to incarceration for nonviolent offenders.

Parole

The practice of releasing prisoners on parole before the end of their sentences has become an integral part of the correctional system in the United States. *Parole* is a variation on imprisonment of convicted criminals. Its purpose is to help individuals reintegrate into society as constructive individuals as soon as they are able, without being confined for the full term of the sentence imposed by the courts. It also serves to lessen the costs to society of keeping an individual in prison. The essence of parole is release from prison, before the completion of sentence, on the condition that **parolees** abide by certain rules during the balance of the sentence. Under some systems, parole is granted automatically after the service of a certain portion of a prison term. Under others, parole is granted by the discretionary action of a board, which evaluates an array of information about a prisoner and makes a prediction whether he is ready to reintegrate into society.

To accomplish the purpose of parole, those who are allowed to leave prison early are subjected to specified conditions for the duration of their parole. These **conditions of parole** restrict their activities substantially beyond the ordinary restrictions imposed by law on an individual citizen. Typically, parolees are forbidden to use alcohol and other intoxicants or to have associations or correspondence with certain categories of undesirable persons (such as felons). Typically, also they must seek permission from their parole officers before engaging in specified activities, such as changing employment or housing arrangements, marrying, acquiring or operating a motor vehicle, traveling outside the community, and incurring substantial indebtedness. Additionally, parolees must regularly report to their **parole officer**.

The parole officers are part of the administrative system designed to assist parolees and to offer them guidance. The conditions of parole serve a dual purpose; they prohibit, either absolutely or conditionally, behavior that is deemed dangerous to the restoration of the individual into normal society. Moreover, through the requirement of reporting to the parole officer and seeking guidance and permission before doing many things, the officer is provided with information about the parolee and an opportunity to advise him. The combination puts the parole officer into the position in which he can try to guide the parolee into constructive development.

The enforcement advantage that supports the parole conditions derives from the authority to return the parolee to prison to serve out the balance of his sentence if he fails to abide by the rules. In practice, not every violation of parole conditions automatically leads to revocation. Typically, a parolee will be counseled to abide by the conditions of parole, and the parole officer ordinarily does not take steps to have parole revoked unless he thinks that the violations are serious and continuing so as to indicate that the parolee is not adjusting properly and cannot be counted on to avoid antisocial activity. The broad discretion accorded the parole officer is also inherent in some of the quite vague conditions, such as the typical requirement that the parolee avoid "undesirable" associations or correspondence. Yet revocation of parole is not an unusual phenomenon, affecting only a few parolees. According to the Supreme Court in *Morrissey v. Brewer*, 35% - 45% of all parolees are subjected to revocation and return to prison. Sometimes revocation occurs when the parolee is accused of another crime; it is often preferred to a new prosecution because of the procedural ease of recommitting the individual on the basis of a lesser showing by the State.

Probation

Probation is very similar to parole, and many of the legal issues are identical. Many jurisdictions combine the job of probation and parole officer, and these officers are often employed in departments of community corrections. The most basic difference between probation and parole is that probationers are sentenced to community sanctions rather than a prison sentence. Parolees have already served at least some prison time. Some jurisdictions can sentence an offender to a split sentence. A **split sentence** requires the offender to stay in prison for a short time before being released on probation.

Most criminal justice historians trace the roots of modern probation to **John Augustus**, who began his professional life as a businessperson and boot maker. Augustus became known as the father of probation largely due to his strong belief in abstinence from alcohol. He was an active member in the Washington Total Abstinence Society, an organization that believed criminals motivated by alcohol could be rehabilitated by human kindness and moral teachings rather than incarceration. His work began in earnest when, in 1841, he showed up in a Boston police court to bail out a "common drunkard." Augustus accompanied the man on his court date three weeks later, and those present were stunned at the change in the man. He was sober and well kempt. For 18 years, he served in the capacity of a probation officer on a purely voluntary basis. Shortly after his death in 1859, a probation statute was passed so that his work could continue under the auspices of the state. With the rise of psychology's influence in the 1920s, probation officers moved from practical help in the field to a more therapeutic model. The pendulum swung back to a more practical bent in the 1960s when probation officers began to act more as service brokers. They assisted probationers with such things as obtaining employment, obtaining housing, managing finances, and getting an education.

Many jurisdictions have several levels of supervision. The most common distinction between levels of probationers is **active supervision** and **inactive supervision**. Probationers on active supervision are required to report in with a probation officer at regular intervals. Probationers can be placed on inactive supervision because they committed only minor offenses. Serious offenders can sometimes be placed on inactive supervision when they have completed much of a long probation sentence without problems.

The preferred method of checking in depends on the jurisdiction. Many require in person visits, but some jurisdictions allow phone calls and checking in via mail. Inactive probationers are not required to check in at all or very infrequently. Checking in with an officer is a condition of probation. Other conditions often include participation in treatment programs, paying fines, and not using drugs or alcohol. If these conditions are not followed, the probationer is said to be a **violator**. Violators are subject to probation **revocation**. Revocations often result in a prison sentence, but some violators are given second chances, and some are sentenced to special programs for **technical violations**. Many jurisdictions classify **absconders** differently than other violators. An absconder is a probationer (or parolee) that stops reporting and "disappears."

Following the trend of mass incarceration in the United States over the past several decades has been a similar trend in what has been called "mass community supervision." In 1980, about 1.34 million offenders were on probation or parole in the United States. That figure exploded to nearly 5 million by 2012. The Bureau of Justice Statistics (Maruschak & Parks, 2014) provides a look at these numbers from a different vantage point: about 1 in 50 adults in the United States were under community supervision at yearend 2012. The community supervision population includes adults on probation, parole, or any other post-prison supervision.

Officer Roles

Many jurisdictions combine the role of probation officer and parole officer into a single job description. In *Gagnon v. Scarpelli* (1973), the court had this to say of the duties of the such officers: "While the parole or probation officer recognizes his double duty to the welfare of his clients and to the safety of the general community, by and large concern for the client dominates his professional attitude. The parole agent ordinarily defines his role as representing his client's best interests as long as these do not constitute a threat to public safety." This statement suggests a dichotomy in the responsibility of parole (and probation) officers; these must look out for the best interest of the client as well as looking out for the best interest of the public. This fact frequently enters into politics. Liberals tend to focus on the treatment and rehabilitation of the offender, and conservatives focus more on the safety of the public and just deserts for the offender.

From the perspective of the parole officers, they must perform law enforcement duties that are designed to protect the public safety. These functions very much resemble the tasks of police officers. They are also officers of the court, and are responsible for enforcing court orders. These orders often include such things as drug testing programs, drug treatment programs, alcohol treatment programs, and anger management programs. Officers are often required to appear in court and give testimony regarding the activities of their clients. They frequently perform searches and seize evidence of criminal activity or technical violations. The courts often ask officers to make recommendations when violations do occur. Officers may recommend that violators be sent to prison, or continue on probation or parole with modified conditions.

There is ambivalence about the role of probation and parole officers within the criminal justice community. This has to do with an artificial dichotomy, often being characterized as police work versus social work. The detection and punishment of law and technical violations are characterized as the law enforcement role. The rehabilitation and reintegration of the offender are regarded as the social work role. Officers tend to lean more heavily toward one of these objectives than the other. Some officers embrace the law enforcement perspective, and seek strict compliance with the law and conditions of parole. Other officers view themselves more as counselors, helping the offender reform, and brokering community resources to help resolve problems. Which model a particular officer exemplifies has many influences. The officer's personal beliefs, the dominate culture of the local office, the policy dictates of agency heads, and legislative enactments driven by political philosophies all play a role in shaping the working personality of each officer. The most effective officers are likely to be hybrids that fall somewhere in between the two archetypes.

Intermediate Sanctions

Traditionally, a person convicted of an offense was sentenced to probation, or sentenced to prison. There was no middle ground. The purpose of intermediate sanctions is to seek that middle ground by providing a punishment that is more severe than probation alone, yet less severe that an period of incarceration. Perhaps the most common among these alternatives is *Intensive Supervision Probation* (ISP). Offenders given to this sort of intermediate sanction are assigned to an officer with a reduced caseload. Caseloads are reduced in order to provide the officer with more time to supervise each individual probationer. Frequent surveillance and frequent drug testing characterize most ISP programs. Offenders are usually chosen for these programs because they have been judged to be at a high risk for reoffending.

Another common type of alternative to prison is the **work release program**. These programs are designed to maintain environmental control over offenders while allowing them to remain in the workforce. Most often, offenders sentenced to a work release program reside in a work release center, which can be operated by a county jail, or be part of the state prison system. Either way, work-release center residents are allowed to leave confinement for work related purposes. Otherwise, they are locked in a secure facility.

Correctional *boot camps* are facilities run along similar lines to military boot camps. Military style discipline and structure along with rigorous physical training are the hallmarks of these programs. Usually, relatively young and nonviolent offenders are sentenced to terms ranging from three to six months in boot camps. Research has found that convicts view boot camps as more punitive than prison, and would prefer prison sentence to being sent to boot camp. Research has also shown that boot camp programs are no more effective at reducing long-term recidivism than other sanctions.

Key Terms

Absconder, Active Supervision, Community Corrections, Conditions of Parole, *Gagnon v. Scarpelli* **(1973), Inactive Supervision, John Augustus, Parole Officer, Parolee, Revocation, Split Sentence, Technical Violation, Violator, Work Release Program**

Learning Objectives

After completing this section, you should be able to:

6.5(a)   Define parole revocation and explain the impact of a revocation on the offender.

6.5(b)   List the major due process rights that violators have at revocation hearings.

6.5(c)   Compare and contrast the Fourth Amendment rights of a probationer (or parolee) with the rights of a suspect not under correctional supervision.

6.5(d)   Describe the limits that the Supreme Court has placed on the conditions of probation (or parole) that lower court judges can require.

6.5(e)   Describe circumstances under which the Court will find conditions of probation (or parole) unconstitutional.

Introduction

For most of the history of probation and parole in the United States, offenders were viewed as having received a gift from the state when they were not sent to prison. Because being on probation or parole was viewed as a privilege conferred by the state, most states believed that they were under no obligation to provide probationers and parolees with the elements of due process they were afforded prior to conviction. In today's legal landscape, the Supreme Court has intervened and now probationers and parolees enjoy some, but not all, of the protections afforded by the Constitution. Note that most of the Supreme Court decisions regarding the rights of probationers and parolees blur the distinction. That is, most of the Court's rulings on probation issues apply to parole as well, and vice versa.

Revocation of Parole

Implicit in the criminal justice system's concern with parole violations is the idea that individuals on parole are entitled to retain their liberty as long as they largely abide by the conditions of parole (or probation). When parolees do fail to live up to these standards, their parole can be revoked. The first step in the **parole revocation** process involves answering a factual question: whether the parolee has in fact acted in violation of one or more conditions of his or her parole. Only if it is determined that the parolee did violate the conditions does the second question arise: should the parolee be recommitted to prison or should other steps be taken to protect society and improve chances of rehabilitation?

The second question involves the application of expertise by the parole authority in making a prediction as to the ability of the individual to live in society without committing antisocial acts. This part of the decision, too, depends on facts, and therefore it is important for the parole board to know not only that some violation was committed but also to know accurately how many and how serious the violations were. Yet this second step, deciding what to do about the violation once it is identified, is not purely factual but also predictive and discretionary.

Parole revocation is very serious for the offender. If a parolee is returned to prison, he or she usually receives no credit for the time "served" on parole. Thus, the violator may face a potential of substantial imprisonment. Revocation deprives an individual, not of the absolute liberty to which every citizen is entitled, but only of the conditional liberty properly dependent on observance of special parole restrictions. This means that the legal standards for parole revocation are not the same as a finding of guilt in criminal court.

Due Process

The liberty of a parolee, although indeterminate, includes many of the core values of unqualified liberty and its termination inflicts a "grievous loss" on the parolee and often on others. Historically, it was common for judges to speak of this problem in terms of whether the parolee's liberty was a "right" or a "privilege." By whatever name, the Supreme Court has determined that liberty is valuable and must be seen as within the protection of the Fourteenth Amendment. Because of this, the courts have determined that its termination calls for some orderly process, however informal.

In *Morrissey v. Brewer* (1972), the Supreme Court refused to write a code of procedure for parole revocation hearings; that, they said, is the responsibility of each State. In this case, the court pointed out that most States have set out procedures by legislation. The Supreme Court did establish a list of minimum due process requirements that must be followed in all revocation proceedings. They include (a) written notice of the claimed violations of parole; (b) disclosure to the parolee of evidence against him; (c) opportunity to be heard in person and to present witnesses and documentary evidence; (d) the right to confront and cross-examine adverse witnesses (unless the hearing officer specifically finds good cause for not allowing confrontation); (e) a "neutral and detached" hearing body such as a traditional parole board, members of which need not be judicial officers or lawyers; and (f) a written statement by the factfinders as to the evidence relied on and reasons for revoking parole.

Specifically, then, *Morrissey* held that a parolee is entitled to two hearings, one a preliminary hearing at the time of his arrest and detention to determine whether there is probable cause to believe that he has committed a violation of his parole, and the other a somewhat more comprehensive hearing prior to the making of the final revocation decision.

In *Gagnon v. Scarpelli* (1973), the court considered the problem of probation revocation hearings. In *Scarpelli*, the court stated:

> Petitioner does not contend that there is any difference relevant to the guarantee of due process between the revocation of parole and the revocation of probation, nor do we perceive one. Probation revocation, like parole revocation, is not a stage of a criminal prosecution, but does result in a loss of liberty. Accordingly, we hold that a probationer, like a parolee, is entitled to a preliminary and a final revocation hearing, under the conditions specified in *Morrissey v. Brewer*.

In *Mempa v. Rhay* (1967), the Court held that a probationer is entitled to be represented by appointed counsel at a combined revocation and sentencing hearing. Reasoning that counsel is required "at every stage of a criminal proceeding where substantial rights of a criminal accused may be affected."

The Fourth Amendment

As with due process rights, a person's Fourth Amendment rights are not nullified just because they are convicted of a crime. What makes probationers and parolees different than the average citizen are their **conditions** of release. Most states require parolees to give up their right to be free from unreasonable searches as part of their conditions. Because the parolee is giving up Fourth Amendment rights, this element is often referred to as a **Fourth waiver**. The rules that govern officer conduct vary from state to state. In some states, an officer must have reasonable suspicion before conducting a probation search. In many states, an officer can conduct a suspicionless search at any time, without reason to believe that the offender committed a new crime. Who may search also varies from jurisdiction to jurisdiction. Some jurisdictions only allow probation and parole officers to search without probable cause, and some extend this authority to police officers as well.

Conditions of Probation and Parole

As previously discussed, offenders are only granted probation or parole if they agree to abide by certain, specified conditions. These can be general conditions that apply to all offenders released in a particular jurisdiction, or they can be tailored to the special needs of a particular offender. The intent of these conditions is to help insure that the dual objectives of control and rehabilitation are met. Because of the fragmented nature of courts in the United States, there is a great deal of variability in the philosophy and practice of imposing these conditions.

The power to impose conditions of probation and parole is most often vested in the courts. Judges have immense discretion when it comes to choosing conditions. Most courts rely on community corrections officers to make suggestions, but the final say us up to the judge. This wide discretion is not, however, without bounds.

Clarity

Recall the *void for vagueness doctrine* discussed in the criminal law chapter. The basis of this legal limit on the power of lawmakers is that it is fundamentally unfair when a reasonable person cannot figure out what exactly a law prohibits. The courts have viewed conditions of probation in the same light. In other words, if the offender cannot figure out what exactly is prohibited because the specification of the condition is too vague, then the condition is unconstitutional. In practice, this means that conditions of probation can vary widely in subject, purpose, and scope, but what is prohibited (or mandated) must be specified in such a way that there is no confusion as to what is required. Conditions that are crafted in vague terms such as "must live honorably" will be struck down by the courts.

Reasonableness

In the context of probation and parole conditions, the term *reasonableness* is often synonymous with *realistic*. The basic requirement is that the conditions set forth by the judge must be such that the offender has the ability to abide by them. If the offender is likely to fail because the conditions cannot possibly be complied with, then the condition will be deemed not reasonable by the courts. It would be unreasonable, for example, to order an indigent offender to pay $10,000 a month in restitution. Addicts have argued that it is unreasonable to expect them to refrain from drug and alcohol use because of the nature of addiction. These claims fail the vast majority of the time. Various courts have reasoned that drug use is illegal, and illegal behavior by probationers and parolees cannot be tolerated.

Related to Protection and Rehabilitation

Since the major goals of probation and parole are to protect society from crime and to rehabilitate the offender, conditions of probation and parole must be reasonably related to one or both of these objectives. If a condition does not relate to these objectives, it will likely be struck down by the courts. In practice, this gives judges very wide latitude in selecting conditions that may be related to these goals. Many courts have struck down conditions of probation that were obviously intended to be "scarlet letter" punishments.

Constitutionality

Several courts have nullified conditions that were contrary to constitutionally protected actions. When constitutional rights are at stake, the government will usually have to establish a compelling state interest in violating the right. In other words, the appellate court will balance the interest the state has in curtailing the right with the cost to the offender. Some rights are afforded greater protection by the court than other rights. These special liberties are often referred to as **fundamental rights**. The freedom of the press, freedom of assembly, freedom of speech, and freedom of religion are among these fundamental rights. For example, courts have struck down conditions that required and offender to attend Sunday school on a regular basis. The court reasoned that forcing someone to participate in a church activity violated the offender's freedom of religion. As previously discussed, Fourth Amendment rights are not nearly so well protected.

Key Terms

Conditions of Release, Fourth Waiver, Fundamental Rights, *Mempa v. Rhay* **(1967),** *Morrissey v. Brewer* **(1972), Parole Revocation**

References

Maruschak, L. M., & Parks, E. (2014). *Probation and Parole in the United States, 2011.* Washington, D.C.: Bureau of Justice Statistics.

ACLU. (2014). *Race and Criminal Justice.* Retrieved July 22, 2014, from The American Civil Liberties Untion: https://www.aclu.org/criminal-law-reform/race-and-criminal-justice

Administrative Office of the U.S. Courts. (2014). *Judical Business of the United States Courts: Annual Report of the Director 2013.* Retrieved June 25, 2014, from United States Courts: http://www.uscourts.gov/Statistics/JudicialBusiness/2013.aspx

American Bar Association. (1986). *Standards on Urban Police Function.* Retrieved November 11, 2013, from American Bar Association Site: http://www.americanbar.org/publications/criminal_justice_section_archive/crimjust_standards_urbanpolice.html

ATF. (2013). *ATF's Mission.* Retrieved November 21, 2013, from Bureau of Alcohol, Tobacco, and Firearms Site: http://www.atf.gov/about/mission.html

Braga, A. A. (2008). *Problem-oriented Policing and Crime Prevention.* Monsey, New York: Criminal Justice Press.

Burch, A. M. (20012, December 6). *Sheriffs' Offices, 2007 - Statistical Tables.* Retrieved November 11, 2013, from Bureau of Justice Statistics: http://www.bjs.gov/index.cfm?ty=pbdetail&iid=4555

Bureau of Justice Statistics. (1993). *Performance Measures for the Criminal Justice System.* Washington, D.C. : Bureau of Justice Statistics.

Bureau of Labor Statistics. (2013). *Occupational Outlook Handbook, 2012-13 Edition.* Washington, D.C.: Bureau of Labor Statistics.

Bureau of the Census. (2014, July 8). *USA Quick Facts.* Retrieved July 22, 2014, from U.S. Bureau of the Census: http://quickfacts.census.gov/qfd/states/00000.html

Cohen, T. H., & Reaves, B. A. (2007). *Pretrial Release of Felony Defendants in State Courts .* Washington, D.C.: Bureau of Justice Statistics .

COPS Office. (2014). *Community Policing Defined.* Washington, D.C. : United States Department of Justice.

Courts, U. S. (2015, July 3). *Defender Services.* Retrieved from United States Courts Site: http://www.uscourts.gov/services-forms/defender-services

Courts, U. S. (2015, July 3). *Probation and Pretrial Services - Mission.* Retrieved from United States Courts: Retrieved from http://www.uscourts.gov/services-forms/probation-and-pretrial-services/probation

DEA. (2013). *DEA Mission Statement.* Retrieved November 21, 2013, from Drug Enforcement Administration Site: http://www.justice.gov/dea/about/mission.shtml

FBI. (2013). *FBI - Quick Facts.* Retrieved November 21, 2013, from Federal Bureau of Investigation Site: http://www.fbi.gov/about-us/quick-facts

FBI. (2015, June 26). *Asset Forfeiture .* Retrieved from FBI Web site: https://www.fbi.gov/about-us/investigate/white_collar/asset-forfeiture

Goldstein, H. (1990). *Problem-oriented Policing .* New York: McGraw Hill.

Harlow, C. W. (2002). *Defense Counsel in Criminal Cases.* Washington : Bureau of Justice Statistics .

Litowitz, D. (1997). Trouble with 'Scarlet Letter' Punishments. *Judicature, 81*(2), 52-57.

Maruschak, L. M., & Bonczar, T. P. (2013). *Probation and Parole in the United States, 2012.* Washington, D.C. : Bureau of Justice Statistics.

NAACP. (2014). *Criminal Justice Fact Sheet.* Retrieved July 22, 2014, from NAACP: http://www.naacp.org/pages/criminal-justice-fact-sheet

Packer, H. L. (1964). Two Models of the Criminal Process. *113 U. Penn. L. Rev. 1* .

We the People of the United States, in Order to form a more perfect Union, establish Justice, insure domestic Tranquility, provide for the common defence, promote the general Welfare, and secure the Blessings of Liberty to ourselves and our Posterity, do ordain and establish this Constitution for the United States of America.

Article. I.

Section. 1.

All legislative Powers herein granted shall be vested in a Congress of the United States, which shall consist of a Senate and House of Representatives.

Section. 2.

The House of Representatives shall be composed of Members chosen every second Year by the People of the several States, and the Electors in each State shall have the Qualifications requisite for Electors of the most numerous Branch of the State Legislature.

No Person shall be a Representative who shall not have attained to the Age of twenty five Years, and been seven Years a Citizen of the United States, and who shall not, when elected, be an Inhabitant of that State in which he shall be chosen.

Representatives and direct Taxes shall be apportioned among the several States which may be included within this Union, according to their respective Numbers, which shall be determined by adding to the whole Number of free Persons, including those bound to Service for a Term of Years, and excluding Indians not taxed, three fifths of all other Persons. The actual Enumeration shall be made within three Years after the first Meeting of the Congress of the United States, and within every subsequent Term of ten Years, in such Manner as they shall by Law direct. The Number of Representatives shall not exceed one for every thirty Thousand, but each State shall have at Least one Representative; and until such enumeration shall be made, the State of New Hampshire shall be entitled to chuse three, Massachusetts eight, Rhode-Island and Providence Plantations one, Connecticut five, New-York six, New Jersey four, Pennsylvania eight, Delaware one, Maryland six, Virginia ten, North Carolina five, South Carolina five, and Georgia three.

When vacancies happen in the Representation from any State, the Executive Authority thereof shall issue Writs of Election to fill such Vacancies.

The House of Representatives shall chuse their Speaker and other Officers; and shall have the sole Power of Impeachment.

Section. 3.

The Senate of the United States shall be composed of two Senators from each State, chosen by the Legislature thereof, for six Years; and each Senator shall have one Vote.

Immediately after they shall be assembled in Consequence of the first Election, they shall be divided as equally as may be into three Classes. The Seats of the Senators of the first Class shall be vacated at the Expiration of the second Year, of the second Class at the Expiration of the fourth Year, and of the third Class at the Expiration of the sixth Year, so that one third may be chosen every second Year; and if Vacancies happen by Resignation, or otherwise, during the Recess of the Legislature of any State, the Executive thereof may make temporary Appointments until the next Meeting of the Legislature, which shall then fill such Vacancies.

No Person shall be a Senator who shall not have attained to the Age of thirty Years, and been nine Years a Citizen of the United States, and who shall not, when elected, be an Inhabitant of that State for which he shall be chosen.

The Vice President of the United States shall be President of the Senate, but shall have no Vote, unless they be equally divided.

The Senate shall chuse their other Officers, and also a President pro tempore, in the Absence of the Vice President, or when he shall exercise the Office of President of the United States.

The Senate shall have the sole Power to try all Impeachments. When sitting for that Purpose, they shall be on Oath or Affirmation. When the President of the United States is tried, the Chief Justice shall preside: And no Person shall be convicted without the Concurrence of two thirds of the Members present.

Judgment in Cases of Impeachment shall not extend further than to removal from Office, and disqualification to hold and enjoy any Office of honor, Trust or Profit under the United States: but the Party convicted shall nevertheless be liable and subject to Indictment, Trial, Judgment and Punishment, according to Law.

Section. 4.

The Times, Places and Manner of holding Elections for Senators and Representatives, shall be prescribed in each State by the Legislature thereof; but the Congress may at any time by Law make or alter such Regulations, except as to the Places of chusing Senators.

The Congress shall assemble at least once in every Year, and such Meeting shall be on the first Monday in December, unless they shall by Law appoint a different Day.

Section. 5.

Each House shall be the Judge of the Elections, Returns and Qualifications of its own Members, and a Majority of each shall constitute a Quorum to do Business; but a smaller Number may adjourn from day to day, and may be authorized to compel the Attendance of absent Members, in such Manner, and under such Penalties as each House may provide.

Each House may determine the Rules of its Proceedings, punish its Members for disorderly Behaviour, and, with the Concurrence of two thirds, expel a Member.

Each House shall keep a Journal of its Proceedings, and from time to time publish the same, excepting such Parts as may in their Judgment require Secrecy; and the Yeas and Nays of the Members of either House on any question shall, at the Desire of one fifth of those Present, be entered on the Journal.

Neither House, during the Session of Congress, shall, without the Consent of the other, adjourn for more than three days, nor to any other Place than that in which the two Houses shall be sitting.

Section. 6.

The Senators and Representatives shall receive a Compensation for their Services, to be ascertained by Law, and paid out of the Treasury of the United States. They shall in all Cases, except Treason, Felony and Breach of the Peace, be privileged from Arrest during their Attendance at the Session of their respective Houses, and in going to and returning from the same; and for any Speech or Debate in either House, they shall not be questioned in any other Place.

No Senator or Representative shall, during the Time for which he was elected, be appointed to any civil Office under the Authority of the United States, which shall have been created, or the Emoluments whereof shall have been encreased during such time; and no Person holding any Office under the United States, shall be a Member of either House during his Continuance in Office.

Section. 7.

All Bills for raising Revenue shall originate in the House of Representatives; but the Senate may propose or concur with Amendments as on other Bills.

Every Bill which shall have passed the House of Representatives and the Senate, shall, before it become a Law, be presented to the President of the United States; If he approve he shall sign it, but if not he shall return it, with his Objections to that House in which it shall have originated, who shall enter the Objections at large on their Journal, and proceed to reconsider it. If after such Reconsideration two thirds of that House shall agree to pass the Bill, it shall be sent, together with the Objections, to the other House, by which it shall likewise be reconsidered, and if approved by two thirds of that House, it shall become a Law. But in all such Cases the Votes of both Houses shall be determined by yeas and Nays, and the Names of the Persons voting for and against the Bill shall be entered on the Journal of each House respectively. If any Bill shall not be returned by the President within ten Days (Sundays excepted) after it shall have been presented to him, the Same shall be a Law, in like Manner as if he had signed it, unless the Congress by their Adjournment prevent its Return, in which Case it shall not be a Law.

Every Order, Resolution, or Vote to which the Concurrence of the Senate and House of Representatives may be necessary (except on a question of Adjournment) shall be presented to the President of the United States; and before the Same shall take Effect, shall be approved by him, or being disapproved by him, shall be repassed by two thirds of the Senate and House of Representatives, according to the Rules and Limitations prescribed in the Case of a Bill.

Section. 8.

The Congress shall have Power To lay and collect Taxes, Duties, Imposts and Excises, to pay the Debts and provide for the common Defence and general Welfare of the United States; but all Duties, Imposts and Excises shall be uniform throughout the United States;

To borrow Money on the credit of the United States;

To regulate Commerce with foreign Nations, and among the several States, and with the Indian Tribes;

To establish an uniform Rule of Naturalization, and uniform Laws on the subject of Bankruptcies throughout the United States;

To coin Money, regulate the Value thereof, and of foreign Coin, and fix the Standard of Weights and Measures;

To provide for the Punishment of counterfeiting the Securities and current Coin of the United States;

To establish Post Offices and post Roads;

To promote the Progress of Science and useful Arts, by securing for limited Times to Authors and Inventors the exclusive Right to their respective Writings and Discoveries;

To constitute Tribunals inferior to the supreme Court;

To define and punish Piracies and Felonies committed on the high Seas, and Offences against the Law of Nations;

To declare War, grant Letters of Marque and Reprisal, and make Rules concerning Captures on Land and Water;

To raise and support Armies, but no Appropriation of Money to that Use shall be for a longer Term than two Years;

To provide and maintain a Navy;

To make Rules for the Government and Regulation of the land and naval Forces;

To provide for calling forth the Militia to execute the Laws of the Union, suppress Insurrections and repel Invasions;

To provide for organizing, arming, and disciplining, the Militia, and for governing such Part of them as may be employed in the Service of the United States, reserving to the States respectively, the Appointment of the Officers, and the Authority of training the Militia according to the discipline prescribed by Congress;

To exercise exclusive Legislation in all Cases whatsoever, over such District (not exceeding ten Miles square) as may, by Cession of particular States, and the Acceptance of Congress, become the Seat of the Government of the United States, and to exercise like Authority over all Places purchased by the Consent of the Legislature of the State in which the Same shall be, for the Erection of Forts, Magazines, Arsenals, dock-Yards, and other needful Buildings;—And

To make all Laws which shall be necessary and proper for carrying into Execution the foregoing Powers, and all other Powers vested by this Constitution in the Government of the United States, or in any Department or Officer thereof.

Section. 9.

The Migration or Importation of such Persons as any of the States now existing shall think proper to admit, shall not be prohibited by the Congress prior to the Year one thousand eight hundred and eight, but a Tax or duty may be imposed on such Importation, not exceeding ten dollars for each Person.

The Privilege of the Writ of Habeas Corpus shall not be suspended, unless when in Cases of Rebellion or Invasion the public Safety may require it.

No Bill of Attainder or ex post facto Law shall be passed.

No Capitation, or other direct, Tax shall be laid, unless in Proportion to the Census or enumeration herein before directed to be taken.

No Tax or Duty shall be laid on Articles exported from any State.

No Preference shall be given by any Regulation of Commerce or Revenue to the Ports of one State over those of another: nor shall Vessels bound to, or from, one State, be obliged to enter, clear, or pay Duties in another.

No Money shall be drawn from the Treasury, but in Consequence of Appropriations made by Law; and a regular Statement and Account of the Receipts and Expenditures of all public Money shall be published from time to time.

No Title of Nobility shall be granted by the United States: And no Person holding any Office of Profit or Trust under them, shall, without the Consent of the Congress, accept of any present, Emolument, Office, or Title, of any kind whatever, from any King, Prince, or foreign State.

Section. 10.

No State shall enter into any Treaty, Alliance, or Confederation; grant Letters of Marque and Reprisal; coin Money; emit Bills of Credit; make any Thing but gold and silver Coin a Tender in Payment of Debts; pass any Bill of Attainder, ex post facto Law, or Law impairing the Obligation of Contracts, or grant any Title of Nobility.

No State shall, without the Consent of the Congress, lay any Imposts or Duties on Imports or Exports, except what may be absolutely necessary for executing it's inspection Laws: and the net Produce of all

Duties and Imposts, laid by any State on Imports or Exports, shall be for the Use of the Treasury of the United States; and all such Laws shall be subject to the Revision and Controul of the Congress.

No State shall, without the Consent of Congress, lay any Duty of Tonnage, keep Troops, or Ships of War in time of Peace, enter into any Agreement or Compact with another State, or with a foreign Power, or engage in War, unless actually invaded, or in such imminent Danger as will not admit of delay.

Article. II.

Section. 1.

The executive Power shall be vested in a President of the United States of America. He shall hold his Office during the Term of four Years, and, together with the Vice President, chosen for the same Term, be elected, as follows

Each State shall appoint, in such Manner as the Legislature thereof may direct, a Number of Electors, equal to the whole Number of Senators and Representatives to which the State may be entitled in the Congress: but no Senator or Representative, or Person holding an Office of Trust or Profit under the United States, shall be appointed an Elector.

The Electors shall meet in their respective States, and vote by Ballot for two Persons, of whom one at least shall not be an Inhabitant of the same State with themselves. And they shall make a List of all the Persons voted for, and of the Number of Votes for each; which List they shall sign and certify, and transmit sealed to the Seat of the Government of the United States, directed to the President of the Senate. The President of the Senate shall, in the Presence of the Senate and House of Representatives, open all the Certificates, and the Votes shall then be counted. The Person having the greatest Number of Votes shall be the President, if such Number be a Majority of the whole Number of Electors appointed; and if there be more than one who have such Majority, and have an equal Number of Votes, then the House of Representatives shall immediately chuse by Ballot one of them for President; and if no Person have a Majority, then from the five highest on the List the said House shall in like Manner chuse the President. But in chusing the President, the Votes shall be taken by States, the Representation from each State having one Vote; A quorum for this Purpose shall consist of a Member or Members from two thirds of the States, and a Majority of all the States shall be necessary to a Choice. In every Case, after the Choice of the President, the Person having the greatest Number of Votes of the Electors shall be the Vice President. But if there should remain two or more who have equal Votes, the Senate shall chuse from them by Ballot the Vice President.

The Congress may determine the Time of chusing the Electors, and the Day on which they shall give their Votes; which Day shall be the same throughout the United States.

No Person except a natural born Citizen, or a Citizen of the United States, at the time of the Adoption of this Constitution, shall be eligible to the Office of President; neither shall any Person be eligible to that Office who shall not have attained to the Age of thirty five Years, and been fourteen Years a Resident within the United States.

In Case of the Removal of the President from Office, or of his Death, Resignation, or Inability to discharge the Powers and Duties of the said Office, the Same shall devolve on the Vice President, and the

Congress may by Law provide for the Case of Removal, Death, Resignation or Inability, both of the President and Vice President, declaring what Officer shall then act as President, and such Officer shall act accordingly, until the Disability be removed, or a President shall be elected.

The President shall, at stated Times, receive for his Services, a Compensation, which shall neither be encreased nor diminished during the Period for which he shall have been elected, and he shall not receive within that Period any other Emolument from the United States, or any of them.

Before he enter on the Execution of his Office, he shall take the following Oath or Affirmation:—"I do solemnly swear (or affirm) that I will faithfully execute the Office of President of the United States, and will to the best of my Ability, preserve, protect and defend the Constitution of the United States."

Section. 2.

The President shall be Commander in Chief of the Army and Navy of the United States, and of the Militia of the several States, when called into the actual Service of the United States; he may require the Opinion, in writing, of the principal Officer in each of the executive Departments, upon any Subject relating to the Duties of their respective Offices, and he shall have Power to grant Reprieves and Pardons for Offences against the United States, except in Cases of Impeachment.

He shall have Power, by and with the Advice and Consent of the Senate, to make Treaties, provided two thirds of the Senators present concur; and he shall nominate, and by and with the Advice and Consent of the Senate, shall appoint Ambassadors, other public Ministers and Consuls, Judges of the supreme Court, and all other Officers of the United States, whose Appointments are not herein otherwise provided for, and which shall be established by Law: but the Congress may by Law vest the Appointment of such inferior Officers, as they think proper, in the President alone, in the Courts of Law, or in the Heads of Departments.

The President shall have Power to fill up all Vacancies that may happen during the Recess of the Senate, by granting Commissions which shall expire at the End of their next Session.

Section. 3.

He shall from time to time give to the Congress Information of the State of the Union, and recommend to their Consideration such Measures as he shall judge necessary and expedient; he may, on extraordinary Occasions, convene both Houses, or either of them, and in Case of Disagreement between them, with Respect to the Time of Adjournment, he may adjourn them to such Time as he shall think proper; he shall receive Ambassadors and other public Ministers; he shall take Care that the Laws be faithfully executed, and shall Commission all the Officers of the United States.

Section. 4.

The President, Vice President and all civil Officers of the United States, shall be removed from Office on Impeachment for, and Conviction of, Treason, Bribery, or other high Crimes and Misdemeanors.

Article III.

Section. 1.

The judicial Power of the United States, shall be vested in one supreme Court, and in such inferior Courts as the Congress may from time to time ordain and establish. The Judges, both of the supreme and inferior Courts, shall hold their Offices during good Behaviour, and shall, at stated Times, receive for their Services, a Compensation, which shall not be diminished during their Continuance in Office.

Section. 2.

The judicial Power shall extend to all Cases, in Law and Equity, arising under this Constitution, the Laws of the United States, and Treaties made, or which shall be made, under their Authority;—to all Cases affecting Ambassadors, other public Ministers and Consuls;—to all Cases of admiralty and maritime Jurisdiction;—to Controversies to which the United States shall be a Party;—to Controversies between two or more States;— between a State and Citizens of another State,—between Citizens of different States,—between Citizens of the same State claiming Lands under Grants of different States, and between a State, or the Citizens thereof, and foreign States, Citizens or Subjects.

In all Cases affecting Ambassadors, other public Ministers and Consuls, and those in which a State shall be Party, the supreme Court shall have original Jurisdiction. In all the other Cases before mentioned, the supreme Court shall have appellate Jurisdiction, both as to Law and Fact, with such Exceptions, and under such Regulations as the Congress shall make.

The Trial of all Crimes, except in Cases of Impeachment, shall be by Jury; and such Trial shall be held in the State where the said Crimes shall have been committed; but when not committed within any State, the Trial shall be at such Place or Places as the Congress may by Law have directed.

Section. 3.

Treason against the United States, shall consist only in levying War against them, or in adhering to their Enemies, giving them Aid and Comfort. No Person shall be convicted of Treason unless on the Testimony of two Witnesses to the same overt Act, or on Confession in open Court.

The Congress shall have Power to declare the Punishment of Treason, but no Attainder of Treason shall work Corruption of Blood, or Forfeiture except during the Life of the Person attainted.

Article. IV.

Section. 1.

Full Faith and Credit shall be given in each State to the public Acts, Records, and judicial Proceedings of every other State. And the Congress may by general Laws prescribe the Manner in which such Acts, Records and Proceedings shall be proved, and the Effect thereof.

Section. 2.

The Citizens of each State shall be entitled to all Privileges and Immunities of Citizens in the several States.

A Person charged in any State with Treason, Felony, or other Crime, who shall flee from Justice, and be found in another State, shall on Demand of the executive Authority of the State from which he fled, be delivered up, to be removed to the State having Jurisdiction of the Crime.

No Person held to Service or Labour in one State, under the Laws thereof, escaping into another, shall, in Consequence of any Law or Regulation therein, be discharged from such Service or Labour, but shall be delivered up on Claim of the Party to whom such Service or Labour may be due.

Section. 3.

New States may be admitted by the Congress into this Union; but no new State shall be formed or erected within the Jurisdiction of any other State; nor any State be formed by the Junction of two or more States, or Parts of States, without the Consent of the Legislatures of the States concerned as well as of the Congress.

The Congress shall have Power to dispose of and make all needful Rules and Regulations respecting the Territory or other Property belonging to the United States; and nothing in this Constitution shall be so construed as to Prejudice any Claims of the United States, or of any particular State.

Section. 4.

The United States shall guarantee to every State in this Union a Republican Form of Government, and shall protect each of them against Invasion; and on Application of the Legislature, or of the Executive (when the Legislature cannot be convened), against domestic Violence.

Article. V.

The Congress, whenever two thirds of both Houses shall deem it necessary, shall propose Amendments to this Constitution, or, on the Application of the Legislatures of two thirds of the several States, shall call a Convention for proposing Amendments, which, in either Case, shall be valid to all Intents and Purposes, as Part of this Constitution, when ratified by the Legislatures of three fourths of the several States, or by Conventions in three fourths thereof, as the one or the other Mode of Ratification may be proposed by the Congress; Provided that no Amendment which may be made prior to the Year One thousand eight hundred and eight shall in any Manner affect the first and fourth Clauses in the Ninth Section of the first Article; and that no State, without its Consent, shall be deprived of its equal Suffrage in the Senate.

Article. VI.

All Debts contracted and Engagements entered into, before the Adoption of this Constitution, shall be as valid against the United States under this Constitution, as under the Confederation.

This Constitution, and the Laws of the United States which shall be made in Pursuance thereof; and all Treaties made, or which shall be made, under the Authority of the United States, shall be the supreme Law of the Land; and the Judges in every State shall be bound thereby, any Thing in the Constitution or Laws of any State to the Contrary notwithstanding.

The Senators and Representatives before mentioned, and the Members of the several State Legislatures, and all executive and judicial Officers, both of the United States and of the several States, shall be bound by Oath or Affirmation, to support this Constitution; but no religious Test shall ever be required as a Qualification to any Office or public Trust under the United States.

Article. VII.

The Ratification of the Conventions of nine States, shall be sufficient for the Establishment of this Constitution between the States so ratifying the Same.

The Word, "the," being interlined between the seventh and eighth Lines of the first Page, The Word "Thirty" being partly written on an Erazure in the fifteenth Line of the first Page, The Words "is tried" being interlined between the thirty second and thirty third Lines of the first Page and the Word "the" being interlined between the forty third and forty fourth Lines of the second Page.

Attest William Jackson Secretary

done in Convention by the Unanimous Consent of the States present the Seventeenth Day of September in the Year of our Lord one thousand seven hundred and Eighty seven and of the Independance of the United States of America the Twelfth In witness whereof We have hereunto subscribed our Names....

Amendment I

Congress shall make no law respecting an establishment of religion, or prohibiting the free exercise thereof; or abridging the freedom of speech, or of the press; or the right of the people peaceably to assemble, and to petition the government for a redress of grievances.

Amendment II

A well regulated militia, being necessary to the security of a free state, the right of the people to keep and bear arms, shall not be infringed.

Amendment III

No soldier shall, in time of peace be quartered in any house, without the consent of the owner, nor in time of war, but in a manner to be prescribed by law.

Amendment IV

The right of the people to be secure in their persons, houses, papers, and effects, against unreasonable searches and seizures, shall not be violated, and no warrants shall issue, but upon probable cause, supported by oath or affirmation, and particularly describing the place to be searched, and the persons or things to be seized.

Amendment V

No person shall be held to answer for a capital, or otherwise infamous crime, unless on a presentment or indictment of a grand jury, except in cases arising in the land or naval forces, or in the militia, when in actual service in time of war or public danger; nor shall any person be subject for the same offense to be twice put in jeopardy of life or limb; nor shall be compelled in any criminal case to be a witness against himself, nor be deprived of life, liberty, or property, without due process of law; nor shall private property be taken for public use, without just compensation.

Amendment VI

In all criminal prosecutions, the accused shall enjoy the right to a speedy and public trial, by an impartial jury of the state and district wherein the crime shall have been committed, which district shall have been previously ascertained by law, and to be informed of the nature and cause of the accusation; to be confronted with the witnesses against him; to have compulsory process for obtaining witnesses in his favor, and to have the assistance of counsel for his defense.

Amendment VII

In suits at common law, where the value in controversy shall exceed twenty dollars, the right of trial by jury shall be preserved, and no fact tried by a jury, shall be otherwise reexamined in any court of the United States, than according to the rules of the common law.

Amendment VIII

Excessive bail shall not be required, nor excessive fines imposed, nor cruel and unusual punishments inflicted.

Amendment IX

The enumeration in the Constitution, of certain rights, shall not be construed to deny or disparage others retained by the people.

Amendment X

The powers not delegated to the United States by the Constitution, nor prohibited by it to the states, are reserved to the states respectively, or to the people.

Fourteenth Amendment

Section 1

All persons born or naturalized in the United States, and subject to the jurisdiction thereof, are citizens of the United States and of the State wherein they reside. No State shall make or enforce any law which shall abridge the privileges or immunities of citizens of the United States; nor shall any State deprive any person of life, liberty, or property, without due process of law; nor deny to any person within its jurisdiction the equal protection of the laws.

Section 2

Representatives shall be apportioned among the several States according to their respective numbers, counting the whole number of persons in each State, excluding Indians not taxed. But when the right to vote at any election for the choice of electors for President and Vice-President of the United States, Representatives in Congress, the Executive and Judicial officers of a State, or the members of the Legislature thereof, is denied to any of the male inhabitants of such State, being twenty-one years of age, and citizens of the United States, or in any way abridged, except for participation in rebellion, or other crime, the basis of representation therein shall be reduced in the proportion which the number of such male citizens shall bear to the whole number of male citizens twenty-one years of age in such State.

Section 3

No person shall be a Senator or Representative in Congress, or elector of President and Vice-President, or hold any office, civil or military, under the United States, or under any State, who, having previously taken an oath, as a member of Congress, or as an officer of the United States, or as a member of any State legislature, or as an executive or judicial officer of any State, to support the Constitution of the United States, shall have engaged in insurrection or rebellion against the same, or given aid or comfort to the enemies thereof. But Congress may by a vote of two-thirds of each House, remove such disability.

Section 4

The validity of the public debt of the United States, authorized by law, including debts incurred for payment of pensions and bounties for services in suppressing insurrection or rebellion, shall not be questioned. But neither the United States nor any State shall assume or pay any debt or obligation incurred in aid of insurrection or rebellion against the United States, or any claim for the loss or emancipation of any slave; but all such debts, obligations and claims shall be held illegal and void.

Section 5

The Congress shall have the power to enforce, by appropriate legislation, the provisions of this article.

CPSIA information can be obtained
at www.ICGtesting.com
Printed in the USA
BVHW011723220821
614859BV00006B/46